Well-Remembered Days

Well-Remembered Days

Eoin O'Ceallaigh's
Memoir of a Twentieth-
Century Catholic Life

Edited by
Sorcha O'Grionnach and Arthur Mathews

MACMILLAN

First published 2001 by Macmillan
an imprint of Macmillan Publishers Ltd
25 Eccleston Place, London SW1W 9NF
Basingstoke and Oxford
Associated companies throughout the world
www.macmillan.com

ISBN 0 333 90162 2 (Hardback)
0 333 90163 0 (Trade Paperback)

3 5 7 9 8 6 4 2

A CIP catalogue record for this book is available from
the British Library.

Typeset by SetSystems Ltd, Saffron Walden, Essex
Printed and bound in Great Britain by
Mackays of Chatham plc, Chatham, Kent

Contents

List of Illustrations   vii

Preface   ix

Well-Remembered Days

1 Before Sellotape   3

2 The Awakening Lamp   34

3 Gorillas in the Mist   51

4 Home Amongst the Clouds   78

5 The Whittling Curtain   95

6 Hurrying Through the Threshold   112

7 Return to Buttery Mountain   136

8 Piper at the Gates of Drumcroom   153

9 Angela's Gnashers   178

10 Through Baltinglass, Darkly   201

Further Reading   209

Glossary for Foreign Readers   211

List of Illustrations

1. My parents circa their wedding day. My mother is the woman on the left.

2. A treasured family heirloom: my father's mug commemorating the centenary of the 1798 rebellion. (Photo copyright Eoin O'Ceallaigh, 2000)

3. The serious, and not-so-serious (!), sides of Gloinn.

4. Two studies of Larry Hoey: at around the time of our first meeting at the 1932 Eucharistic Congress (back row, second right), and in later life, on a horse.

5. An explanation of 'The Prayer Crusade', from the official Eucharistic Congress programme.

6. Cardinal MacRory. He surprised me with his Al Jolson impression!

7. Our wedding day, 1933. The happy bride and groom to the right of the picture.

8. Ernest Blythe. A funny incident involving a rabbit almost ended in tragedy for the Abbey Theatre supremo. (Hulton Getty)

9. Our dog 'Festy', who died when he licked fluid from Noreen's knee.

10. Lourdes 1964. 'Ready for take-off!'

11. Gloinn took this snap of me and Maire on the plane. Due to a double exposure, the 'ghost-like' figure of Father Joe Collins is also present! (Note: Maire's face was later scratched out by Gloinn after one of their many arguments)

12. Noreen was fascinated by these straws in a glass.

13. Eamon de Valera. (Bert Hardy / Hulton Getty)

14. Hitler. (Hulton Getty)

15. Gay Byrne. (RTE Ireland)

16. Pope John Paul II. (Hulton Getty)

The Gathering Gust

It is an extraordinary experience to write a book exclusively about oneself. I hope that in these pages I have been as honest about my faults as I have been about my achievements, and that the many colourful, heroic and downright ordinary people gathered together here will thank me if I have portrayed them fairly, and not condemn me if I have seen fit to 'have a go' at them, whether for a genuine reason, or on account of an unjustified personal grudge or prejudice on my part.

The germ of the idea for this book dates back a couple of years ago to a beautiful summer evening in Connemara. I was visiting my good friend Gloinn McTire, who had just finished his ninth book, *The Awakening Lamp* (a title I have appropriated for Chapter 2 of this autobiography). We sat out in the garden of his delightful whitewashed cottage as his wife Maire (at the time recovering from operations on both of her eyes for unrelated disorders) cut the lawn nearby with a pair of blunt shears. I have known Gloinn since he was fifteen and I was twelve years of age, and he figures prominently in these pages. I think in all the years we have known one another we have had only one serious argument; surprisingly enough, over the vexed subject of genital mutilation, a subject which he knows practically nothing about, though typically holds very forthright opinions. Apart from my dear late wife, Noreen, and the saint-like figure of Larry Hoey (whom you will also meet in my story) no one I know, or have known, has been more of an influence on my life than 'Mr McT'. I always say about Gloinn that he has the patience of Mother Theresa mixed with the charisma of Hitler, but these are only two of his numerous qualities. (Without sounding immodest, I like to think that I have influenced him too, not least in his distaste for Protestants.) We both share a distrust of modernization and all its inherent evils, and as we chatted away on that summer evening, he suggested that my memories of Ireland long ago would make a wonderful book. He had planned his own autobiography, but felt sure that his worsening arthritis would make the job impossible. (He has since finished his twelfth novel, *The Brandished Fork*, and thanks the power of prayer for the miraculous newfound suppleness in his fingers. I am inclined to think it may also have something to do with a cutback on his consumption of Jameson's whiskey!)

Encouraged by Gloinn's words, I set to work the following autumn, and had a first draft finished within three months. My daughter Sorcha, whom I entrusted to edit these words, encouraged me throughout, and even, after weeks of argument, allowed me to break with tradition and give this preface its own title, 'The Gathering Gust'. ('You can't do that, Daddy!' – I could, and I did.)

I thank her, as I thank you, for your interest in my experiences along life's highway. May God bless you as He has blessed me.

Eoin O'Ceallaigh
St Columbana's Nursing Home
Oughterard, Co Galway
December 2000.

Well-Remembered Days

Eoin O'Ceallaigh's
Memoir of a Twentieth-
Century Catholic Life

CHAPTER 1

Before Sellotape

In 1997, as part of research for a book I was working on at the time, I found myself sitting in the living room of a clerical friend of mine, Father Bunny Long (also my co-author on the project), watching a videotape entitled '1,001 Blow Jobs'. It was a cheaply made film entertainment emanating from the Far East, and, as the title infers, it featured footage of men and women, most of whom were malnourished orientals, indulging in the sordid 'fun activity' of oral gratification. To his great credit, Father Long – a man in his seventies, who has spent most of his life working as parish priest in the village of Dowerglass in County Limerick – despite being in obvious distress, soldiered on through the disturbing video with a grim determination to 'get the job done'. While the furious images of 'yellow mickeys' (his colourful, and no-doubt racist, description) flickered before him, he made copious notes while resisting what must have been an overwhelming temptation to press the fast-forward button and have the whole grisly business over with. I myself admit to having watched with a feeling of embarrassment and unease, not so much for myself, or indeed my clerical co-viewer, but rather for mankind in general. When the tape finally ended, Bunny switched off the television and turned to me with a look of sorrow on his kindly face. 'Eoin,' he said, 'there was a lot of sex in that film; but do you know what? – I didn't see much love.' He was so right. There was scarcely any real affection evident in any of the blow jobs. It is a theme that has been trumpeted often by the Church in recent years; the emptiness of the sexual act when it takes place without love (e.g. outside marriage). What I remember from the time of my youth is the polar opposite of this sad situation: love without sex. It is a thought that has occurred to me more than once while I was planning this book, and is, I think, a useful starting-off point for my earliest days.

Was it really so long ago? My first memory, like so many children, is of a doting mother. I must have been no more than two or three minutes old. I remember, or at least I think I can remember – surely memory for a child of less than an hour old is hardly possible – looking at a woman's pale grey eyes (for many years afterwards I would associate eyes with women) and taking in the unfamiliar surroundings with a sense of foreboding that is the lot of the newborn. I remember seeing a chair and wondering what it was. There had been nothing remotely like a chair, or indeed any type of household furniture, in my mother's womb, where I was very unfamiliar with any type of hard object. (Although of course, as my friend Gloinn McTire later remarked, it was as a result of a 'hard object' being introduced into the general vicinity that I had come about at all!) The mystery of the chair was soon cleared up when my father sat down in it, and from that moment on, their purpose became clear to me. I would sit down on many over the coming years, often to relax, but more commonly for work purposes.

I had been instigated by a random sexual act (the details of which, when I found out later, sickened me) the previous March, and had duly arrived in November, the coldest month for a hundred years. It had been so cold, I was told later, that my grandfather's eyes had frozen open, and he had been unable to blink for weeks. His neighbours, as neighbours did in those days, helped out, and mimicked a blinking action for him by occasionally holding up rectangular squares of black cardboard in front of his face, so that his vision would be impaired by momentary relieving outbreaks of blackness. Their kindliness, so representative of the good neighbourliness of simple people, impressed me when I later learned of it.

I knew from the very moment of my conception that I would be born into a fabulous environment, and that the next few years of infancy would be nothing short of idyllic.

The novelist Frank McCourt has famously made his fortune in recent years by recalling his childhood days in Athlone at the turn of the century.* His first book of memoirs caused much of a stir by portraying the people of the town as basically a bunch of shiftless, brain-dead peasant wankers

* Editor's note: actually Limerick in the 1930s and 1940s.

living in conditions more reminiscent of the Stone Age than the early twentieth century. He even criticizes the weather, which is depicted in the book as being consistently awful; with McCourt and his fellow slum-dwellers living in freezing Arctic-like temperatures whilst under a constant deluge of rain, hail and sleet as they huddle together praying in their mud cabins. (Needless to say, and all too predictably, as in most modern novels, McCourt also portrays the clergy as child-molesting clowns with a fondness for drink and gambling.) Nobody comes out of the book looking well, and any Irish person who stays at home instead of legging it off to America (like McCourt) is basically seen as being mad. Americans, of course, are portrayed as much more intelligent than the Irish: able to act in films, excelling at maths and foreign languages, having superior communication skills, and generally being much more sophisticated than the poor ignorant Athlone people. Americans, according to McCourt, are just great, while the Irish are a bunch of thuggish morons. This is a very one-sided view, and I think the criticism levelled at McCourt has been justified. My own memory of Ireland in those years is that everyone in the country was blissfully happy all the time. The poverty that McCourt harps on about was confined to a handful of malcontents (probably no more than ten or twelve), who, if pressed, would probably admit that their lot was not so bad after all. The weather was certainly much better than McCourt remembers it, and the people of that era were generally a lovely bronzed colour as a result of working out in the fields under the hot sun. When travelling abroad, Irish men and women were often mistaken for being Spanish. I

remember people *smiled* more, but of course McCourt uses this fact to portray the Irish as gormless imbeciles of the type portrayed by John Mills in the film *Von Ryan's Express*.* No, Frank, they were smiling because they were *happy*, an emotion I'm sure you are unfamiliar with, despite the fact that you have over a million pounds.

Some years ago, my daughter Sorcha, for my eightieth birthday, gave me a facsimile copy of the front page of *The Irish Independent* for the day I was born, November 16th, 1912, which proves beyond question that Ireland in those days was brilliant. Many of the stories in the edition certainly confirm that view. One report in particular caught my eye, because it describes just the kind of incident that couldn't possibly happen nowadays. A 'Mr Devlin from Wicklow' was travelling as a passenger on the mail boat from Dublin to Holyhead, when he leaned over the side to get a closer look at a giant wave. He must have got too close to the wave, however, because his eye glasses were swept overboard. He alerted one of the stewards to his loss, who, in turn, informed the captain, John Moynihan. Captain Moynihan immediately brought the ship to a halt and promised Mr Devlin that the vessel wouldn't move another inch until the glasses were recovered. Of course, nowadays there'd be a riot from the other passengers, most of whom would no doubt be on their way to Old Trafford to see Manchester United play Liverpool, and would cry into their

* Editor's note: actually *Ryan's Daughter*.

overpriced replica jerseys if they missed the first five minutes. But back then no one minded a short delay if it was in order to help a fellow traveller. The captain sent three of his crew overboard to see if by any chance the glasses were still floating on the surface, but they returned empty-handed. Moynihan then realized that the missing 'specs' had probably sunk to the bottom, and were now lying somewhere on the seabed. He himself volunteered for the difficult job of locating them, despite the fact that he had no expertise *at all* in the highly specialized procedure of recovering objects from the bottom of the sea. To hinder his plan further, no diving equipment of any description could be found on board. (It is also worth noting that the passenger steamer, *The Marita-Ann*, had sunk in the same waters the previous year, and no trace had been found of her. If a big boat like that couldn't be located, there must have been little chance of finding a pair of spectacles.) Nevertheless, the captain was obviously a determined man, and he pressed ahead with his plan by improvising a makeshift underwater suit out of an old boiler suit and a goldfish bowl. (He was aided in this task by a 'Miss Heatherington from Surrey; a seamstress returning from a visit to Irish relatives'.) Moynihan then jumped over the side, to 'loud cheers from the passengers and cries of encouragement from the crew', but, alas, never re-emerged. Two more deckhands subsequently died in a failed rescue attempt, and the glasses were not recovered. I find it a most heartwarming story, illustrating once again the selflessness of people of the time, and the importance of giving the customer good service, despite the risk of personal discomfort or, as in this case, death. I think this 'customer is always right' ethos is something many of our state and semi-state companies could learn from today.*

My father John O'Kelly, who never had any time for bad service, was thirty-two when I was born. Although originally from Kerry, one day, as a very young child, he had started following a horse outside his front door and ended up in Dublin. He liked the bright (paraffin) lights of the city and pursued a series of odd jobs in the capital.

My mother was an O'Regan from Clare. From her I got my great love of the Irish language, which I have always thought is probably the best language in the world. She was from a family of sixteen, all girls: fifteen of whom were extremely beautiful – the sad exception being the dowdy and unattractive figure of Auntie Maud – and all proudly nationalist. I can never recall Mammy wearing anything other than a white blouse and a darkly coloured, pleated skirt. I never once in my life saw her knees. Her hair, which was the blackest I've ever seen – until it turned white overnight in the late 1960s after seeing an edition of *Top of the Pops* – was always tightly tied behind her head in a neatly packed shiny black bun that resembled a rather wiry-looking snooker ball. (Although, of course, it would very much test the ability of a Dennis Taylor or a Steven Hendry to make a break of a hundred and forty, at the World Snooker Cham-

* An interesting footnote: Mr Devlin subsequently sued the mail-boat company for the loss of his glasses.

pionships at the Crucible in Sheffield using my mother's hairy bun!)

Mammy had originally moved to Dublin at the age of fifteen to work as a maid in the house of a Mr Connolly, a signwriter, who had made his fortune during the first burst of enthusiasm for 'Exit' signs. (Before then, people would always have to ask, 'Is this the way out?') He lived in a large house in Howth with his three sons, and my mother became very close to the boys. The youngest, Colm, subsequently became the first Irish motorist convicted under the drink-driving act (the first of many!). As a result, his father, broken-hearted, turned to porter for comfort, and before long the entire family, like so many Irish families, had succumbed to the indignities of alcoholism.

I myself, I am happy to say, have never developed a taste for the porter, or any type of alcoholic drink. I have seen the bad effect it has on many people's lives, not least, on my old friend Gloinn McTire. People who drink often have a very peculiar attitude to us non-drinkers. They think we're 'stuffy' or that we 'don't enjoy a laugh'. I love a laugh, but I can have just as much of a laugh without drinking. The difference is that I don't wake up the next morning with a sore head. I never met anyone who gets up out of their bed after a night on the town and says, 'Oh, I wish I'd had another drink last night. That would have been a great idea.' I have found that I can have as much fun as anyone when I'm in a pub by just sipping a 7-Up (accompanied by an occasional bag of cheese'n'onion crisps). It's cheap as well, as one 7-Up would usually last me the whole night. The Irish in my opinion – and I don't like to say it – have an irresponsible attitude to alcohol. When I've been abroad, I have lost count of the number of people (seven or eight thousand?) who have come up to me and said, 'The Irish are great fun and they have a tremendous sense of humour, but why, oh *why* do they have to drink so much?'

A great pal of mine, Father Sean Fagan, who despite his Irish sounding name is actually a genuine Cherokee Indian from Wyoming (he had a bit part in the film *Dances with Wolves*), is also puzzled by this phenomenon. When I visit him in his parochial house in New Jersey, he always enjoys a glass of sherry in the evening; in fact he often says during the course of the day – with a very mischievous look on his face! – 'I'm looking forward to the old glass of sherry, Eoin, I don't mind admitting!' But when his duties are completed and he is able to put his feet up and relax, he contents himself with 'just the one'. He doesn't need to go drinking a crate full of the stuff. He says that it's very sad to see many of the Irish priests he knows with drink problems, and that he prays for them every day. While I wouldn't go so far as to say that every Irish priest has a drink problem, it's fair to say that a percentage of them (perhaps 99 per cent) do suffer in this regard. Hopefully, due in no small part to the ending of duty-free facilities, things will change in this area in the next few years, especially if the legislation ever extends to the Dublin/Boston run.

It was towards the end of 1909, just as the novelty of the new century was wearing off, that my parents met each other, and it was, it must be said, under most peculiar circumstances. My mother, to her husband's great embarrassment, never tired of telling the tale. It seemed that my father had sat on a toilet seat and become very worried that he had contracted a sexual disease. Nowadays, of course, we know that it's practically impossible to contract VD (or 'The Splatters', as it was known in Dublin at the time) from toilet seats, but this was a very different era, and ignorance was still rife. Knowing that Mr Connolly had several encyclopedias showing graphic pictures of diseased sexual parts, my father paid a visit to him for a 'look at the books'. Mr Connolly suggested that if he was worried, it might be a good idea to take his trousers down, and compare his member to some of the pictures. This my father did, to the amusement of both men. Inevitably, some good-natured horseplay ensued, and things were just about to get a little out of hand when my mother popped her head round the door of the library. Luckily, she got a rear view of the situation, and at least some of my father's modesty was preserved. My mother later confessed to my sister, Grainne, that she had never got the full 'front view' in nearly fifty years of marriage. How different things are these days, when 'full frontal' panoramas of one's partner are regarded as a normal part of everyday life. Indeed, if you don't get a regular close-up 'eyeful' of your partner's genitals, people think there is something wrong with you.

My father's father, my grandfather, was a larger-than-life character. His wife, my grandmother, had died in one of the first dynamite explosions in Ireland. My grandfather had been scarred in the same incident, and much of his face was attached to his head by strange contraptions that looked like pipe cleaners. A huge gash, a result of almost being split in two in another accident, ran from between his legs to the top of his head on both the front and back of his body, and left him in excruciating and unbearable pain for most of his life. But despite this – in fact maybe even because of it – he was always in 'great form', and we eagerly looked forward to our regular visits to him. He lived in Dolphin's Barn, not very far away from us in the Liberties. He had a very small room (four feet by two feet) in a tenement building there, and always complained about the cold. In fact, he had a great interest in the cold, and one of his main pastimes was recording chilly temperatures. Every day he would buy *The Freeman's Journal*, look up the previous day's temperature, and if it was between 0 and 40 degrees Fahrenheit, he would make a note of it in a special jotter he kept under his bed. If the temperature was over 40 degrees, he would furrow his brow and make a disappointed 'tut-tut' sound, but after a few moments he would be resigned to the situation and would mumble a simple 'never mind'. He doted on his three grandchildren: myself, Grainne and Brian, and would bounce us up and down on his knees with great force, often causing us to hit the ceiling. (Subsequently, Brian has discovered in recent years that he is mildly brain damaged). Granddaddy's big claim to fame was that he had met Parnell ('the Unborn King of Ireland'), and believed him to be the greatest Irishman that had ever lived. However, my grandfather was a devout Catholic and turned against Parnell after the split within the Irish Parliamentary Party over the Kitty O'Shea affair. This caused the old man great sadness, but he felt that in matters of conscience his own thoughts were of absolutely no consequence at all. My father was an equally staunch Catholic, and I'd like to think that my own devotion to the Church is as unswerving, unquestioning and unthinking as the previous generations of O'Ceallaighs.

My grandfather once told me an interesting story about Parnell. Even though he was a hugely popular politician and adored by the Irish people, he was very self-conscious about going bald. You can see, in the relatively few photographs that exist of him, that he tends to tilt his head away from the camera. Probably he was aware that the flash from the photographer's bulb would cause light to bounce harshly off his thinning pate. The story goes that he was electioneering in Clonmel once when an old crone, reputed to be a local 'wise woman', approached him and promised that she could cure his premature hair loss by rubbing a mixture of salt and sand into it. Parnell told her to 'feck off'.

Our house in the Liberties was not large, but to us children it was a 'palace of delights'. I was the eldest child, born in 1912, and Grainne and Brian followed in 1914 and 1916 respectively. Brian in fact was a twin, born with Enda, but Enda was lost after a few days, and we never found him again. My parents did make a half-hearted search for him, but basically, he'd just gone off – Grainne said later it was possibly to see if he could get himself hitched up to a better family! – and that was it. (No doubt if such an incident happened today, the parents would be jailed for negligence, but in those days people just thought 'so what'.)

I still retain many, many vivid images from my child-hood. I remember very clearly a huge dresser in the kitchen bedecked with huge plates, cup, saucers, and mugs. My father had a very special mug dating from 1898 commemorating the great rebellion of a century before, depicting brave 'Father Murphy from old Kilcor-mack', one of the patriotic insurgents whose name has passed gloriously down through the generations. 'Look at him there on the mug,' my father used to say, point-ing out the sad figure of a very frightened Father Mur-phy, naked from the waist down, his buttocks in ribbons after having taken an unmerciful whipping from the hard-faced Redcoat standing sternly over him. 'Poor ould Father Murphy,' my father would remark sadly, 'he's a great reminder of the hatred that the British always had for the Catholic people of Ireland.' The mug is still in my possession.

There was little entertainment in those days, but once or twice a year our parents would take us to the Hilarity Theatre in Dame Street to see some of the popular variety acts of the day perform in the annual Children's Christmas Show. I remember very well seeing one of the most famous

entertainers of the day, Barney Walsh, 'The Coal-Coloured Nig Nog', in the show of 1918. Barney's act wouldn't be allowed into any theatre these days as even to a six-year-old boy like me it seemed somewhat racist. Basically, he would come on stage, completely blacked-up in shoe polish, and launch into a ferocious attack against anyone who was a member of an ethnic minority. His catchphrase, which he must have yelled out about a hundred times during his performance, was 'Yez are all feckin' Zulus!' He wasn't even that funny. Amongst the other artists I remember was Harry Metcalf, who had made his debut on the Dublin stage as a five-year-old at the time of the Great Famine doing humorous impressions of the starving. I don't think his act had changed much over the years, and it seemed somewhat out of place in the Dublin of 1918. (It was also rather tasteless – he'd probably make a fortune on today's 'alternative-comedy' circuit.) You either 'have it' or you 'don't' and Harry certainly 'didn't'. Eileen Dunning, 'The Singing Canary', sang operatic arias in a bath filled with flowers and empty champagne bottles. She was very poor value for money indeed. Nevertheless, I would have to add that even though all these acts were appallingly bad, they were still much better than anything you'd see nowadays.

The household chores for my mother were endless. Every day, the dust would have to be sifted, sorted into piles and distributed evenly throughout the house. For instance, the dust from the bedroom would be put into bags, brought down to the parlour and emptied, while the dust from the parlour would be similarly removed to the bedroom. The cataloguing alone for this procedure took several hours. Due to the damp walls, all the wallpaper in the house usually had to be replaced on a daily basis, while a large part of the evenings would be spent holding on to the chimney to stop it falling down. Mammy would also have to trap and kill the rats that lived under the kitchen sink and bake fifteen or sixteen loaves of bread a day whilst breast feeding not only Brian, Grainne and myself, but also the children of neighbours, and Mr O'Brien, a local schoolteacher who paid her a shilling for the experience. She did all this uncomplainingly, usually whilst whistling one of Moore's popular Irish melodies.

I recall very clearly a coal scuttle beside the fire which doubled as a bath. I have no memory of a lavatory. This is because we didn't have one. We had an outside facility located an hour's journey away by tram, and 'a need to go' in the middle of the night was always a thing to be dreaded. Even today, being 'caught short' can be a sobering experience, and later on in my story I shall tell of an incident that occurred while I was chaperoning the Papal Nuncio at the 1989 Rose of Tralee festival which left both the Nuncio and myself with much egg on our faces.

As a child I enjoyed reading sagas of ancient Irish legends. I was enthralled by tales of MacNubh and the Otters; of Conor MacSloidh, the hasty copper manufacturer of Cong and his battles with Deirdreen of the Songs ('she of the Medium-Tempo Ballad' as Speranza, the folklorist and

mother of Oscar Wilde, described her); of Saint Patrick, who has given his name to a national holiday, a football club and a mental institution; and Saint Brendan, who discovered the United States three weeks before Columbus. One story I remember hearing from Mammy was about Finn Og MacOngasairt, a genuine living legend of his era, who had an altercation with Art of the Four Eyes, one of the first Irish mythological heroes to wear glasses. Finn mocked Art for his shortsightedness, and for his teasing was thrown over the edge of a cliff. But instead of drowning in the sea, Finn clung on to a rock, and when the tide went out, he climbed back up. He surprised Art when he was at his toilet, and poked his eyes out with a branch from a tree. This made Art furious, and he tied Finn up with a length of rope, beat him senseless, and (as if that wasn't enough!) hacked his feet off. Certainly, one could refer to this as an early example of a 'punishment beating'. (Who knows, maybe even Finn had to leave the country within twenty-four hours after being threatened by a Stone Age version of Martin McGuinness!) Possibly a ferocious dragon also became involved at that point (my memory is a little vague) and the whole affair ended with everybody lying in a bloody heap on the ground. Of course, there were no emergency services or ambulances in those days to come and take them away, so they all had to just lie there in agony until they died. If something like that happened today there would no doubt be an article in *The Guardian* by Fergal Keane relating the events to his son's birthday party, and a benefit concert for the relatives organized by Bono of U2. However, in ancient times, incidents like these

were not seen as anything out of the ordinary, and would hardly even warrant a mention in the newspapers of the day. This type of story strengthened my sense of Irish identity even further, and I knew I was destined to follow in my family's nationalist tradition.

My first memories of Dublin are happy ones, but to the citizen of the twenty-first century they would be unfamiliar relics of a gentler time. There was little traffic, and the streets of the city were full of horses. In the Liberties, old nags (no, I don't mean the elderly ladies!) pulled carts for the many breweries, bakeries and creameries (no, I don't mean the massage parlours!) in the area. As youngsters, we would often climb up on the back of the carts, to the irate protests of the hapless driver. I remember once climbing on to a cart with my friend Shinty Bolger. We were probably nine or ten years old at the time. The old man who drove bread to and from the local bakery* (I could never understand why he drove bread *to* the bakery) was a very grumpy individual, and was driven mad by us young 'uns. We called him 'Old Misery Trousers'. He would always yell at us and threatened to tell our parents about our cart-hopping activities. But this day Shinty had an extra special surprise in store for the old codger. Shinty's father had fought in the Boer war, and still had a rifle bayonet from that time. Well, lo and behold, hadn't Shinty brought the weapon with him. We leapt on to the back as usual, when the cart

* Now, sadly, a Gay and Lesbian Visitors Centre.

stopped at a T-junction halfway between the bakery and Shinty's house. 'Get off my cart, you f*****g c***s!' yelled old Misery Trousers as we scrambled on. But before he could protest any more, Shinty sliced off the old man's ear with the bayonet and then ate it right in front of his eyes! Blood was everywhere, and Shinty was laughing his head off. The look of confusion and terror on the old timer's face was genuinely hilarious. There was always fun like that to be had, and I can remember many incidents which even now can bring tears of laughter to my eyes.

When I was not yet four years old, a momentous event occurred in Dublin. This of course was the 1916 Rising. Already, the 1914–1918 war was raging in Europe, and many Irishmen had gone to 'The Front', a pub on the quays, where they would discuss the latest news from the battlefields and argue about the rights and wrongs of volunteering for service. At first, as has been well documented, there was great enthusiasm for the gallant crusade to free little Belgians. Nowadays, we are all very familiar with the newsreels of the period showing the brave troops frantically waving hankies from trains and smiling excitedly at the cameras. It just somehow didn't occur to people at the time, least of all the soldiers, that anyone would end up getting killed, despite the fact that the event had been plainly billed as a war.

At home, there was much talk of the Irish nationalist revival, and many people had joined organizations such as the Gaelic League, which was intent on restoring the ancient native tongue to everyday use. Although the Gaelic language was to all intents and purposes as extinct as the dinosaurs, it was being enthusiastically embraced – largely in an effort to annoy the British – and it was a common sight to see members of the patriotic Irish Volunteers drilling on the streets and talking very basic Irish to each other (mostly phrases such as 'May I go to the toilet?' and 'The cat ran into the box'). However, it was still a surprise to learn of the capture of the General Post Office by rebels on that Easter weekend. Up until that point, the Post Office was mainly known as a place you'd go to to buy stamps. Our home was fiercely nationalist, and I begged my father to allow me to join the fighting men in Sackville (now O'Connell) Street. He told me that I'd only get in the way – as I have said, at this time I was not yet four years old – and that I could assist the rebels best by praying for them. I asked if there was any chance that I could offer my services as some kind of distraction, but I was unclear as to what I meant by this, and so was my father. It was a very vague idea, and I didn't really know what I was on about. To confuse the issue even further, my father told me years later that I had also enquired about pay and conditions.

After the fighting had ended and the insurgents surrendered, I accompanied my parents into the centre of town to see the destruction in the aftermath of the fighting. Walking along the quays, I remember looking into the River Liffey (at that time one of the oldest rivers in the world) and seeing a badly wounded swan and some ducks who looked more than a little annoyed that their tranquil aquatic existence had been disturbed by a noisy rebellion. When we arrived at Sackville Street, there was smoke and debris everywhere, and the Post Office lay in ruins. I saw a horse's head, his eyes still blinking, lying in the middle of the street with no sign of his body anywhere. He obviously didn't know what the hell was going on. One minute he had been trotting down Sackville Street with a lancer on his back, the next his head was being blown off. Bystanders in the street gazed in disbelieving wonder at the ruins. I remember tears in my father's eyes, and Mother asking him why he was so upset. Not wishing to appear 'soft', my father said that he was crying because he had a pain in his balls. But I knew that he felt a tremendous respect for the great sacrifice that had been made on behalf of the Irish people, and his tears showed a great reverence for the suffering of the rebel leader Padraig Pearse and his men.

The Rising had not been popular with the ordinary people (nor, indeed, the animals!) of Dublin, but after the executions of the leaders the mood changed, and a strong feeling of nationalism emerged. Soon, violence gripped the land in the shape of a bloody conflict between the Irish Republican Army and the Black and Tans. The 'Tans' were very unpopular in the country, and their wickedness has gone down in the annals of Irish history. When people today ask me how unpopular they really were, I always reply 'very unpopular'. In any poll taken to find out the most popular military force ever to suppress Ireland, there's no way they'd finish anywhere near the top ten.

A great-aunt of mine, a saintly nun who wouldn't hurt a fly, suffered at their hands in a terrible way. I have always had great reverence for nuns since I was educated by them in my earliest years, and no words can adequately describe the abhorrence I still feel when I recall this dreadful incident. My great-aunt, then aged well over eighty years of age (some reports put her at nearly a hundred), had been to visit an old priest in the country and was making her way back to Dublin when she was stopped by a Tan patrol near Ashbourne. After making fun of her accent and calling her 'Paddy' (which was bizarre, as she was a very old nun), one of these loutish cockneys then did something unspeakably awful. It was only weeks later that she was able to tell the Mother Superior in her convent what had happened; the sick 'Tan' had shamelessly taken down his breeches and done a 'shite' in front of her. Even by today's standards, when we have grown wearily used to the exploits of people like the footballer Paul Gascoigne, the incident seems truly shocking. I have often imagined the scene on that lonely road near Ashbourne; the leering face of the Tan contrasting sharply with the awestruck horror which suddenly comes over the serenely spiritual face of my great-aunt as the drama unfolds before her. And, of course, this type of thing went on all the time. With behaviour like that, it was no wonder that the men of the old IRA enjoyed great support from the people of

Ireland. Heroes like Dan Breen or Ernie O'Malley would no sooner have done something like that in front of a nun than they would kick an archbishop or be filmed by the newsreel cameras of the time performing oral sex.

During 1920, the Tan war escalated, and it was during that fateful year that I came into contact with the great Michael Collins.

'What was he really like?' people often ask me when they know that I met Collins. I reply that he was everything that the history books say about him. By turns brave and gentle, ruthless and kind, kind and brave, gentle and ruthless; he was a true hero in our family. Later, my parents would come to disagree with Collins's politics, but in the days before 1922 a bad word about 'the Big Fella' was never uttered in our house. He met my father through a mutual friend, Batty Ginnity, who had been interned in Frongoch camp in Wales with Collins after the Easter Rising. Ginnity was a giant of a man from Longford, and knew of my father's nationalist leanings. One day he asked Daddy if he would be willing to do something for 'the cause'. My father immediately replied 'yes', with the proviso that he didn't wish to become involved if there was any risk of breaking the law or offending the British authorities in any way. When he was told that he would be required to shoot people, he reluctantly declined. However, within six months, he had the chance to do his patriotic duty for the country. It was during a warm spell of weather, and it was known that we had a particularly cool larder. I well remember Ginnity coming round with a small parcel of sausages and wondering if we could keep them cold for him for a couple of days. (There was some initial confusion, as my father had thought at first that Batty had said 'spermicides'.) My mother was very puzzled at this request. It was well known that Batty had a large and cool larder himself; in fact, he had recently won an award presented by the Lord Mayor at the Dublin Show in recognition of the 'outstanding largeness and coolness' of his larder. There was a long discussion, but finally the old internee became impatient and gave us an ultimatum: 'Are you going to hide the sausages or not?' My father, perhaps influenced by a photograph of Padraig Pearse's profile on the wall, said yes. Ginnity was noticeably relieved. However, we were still not quite sure why we had to hide the parcel. But as he was going out the door, the Longford giant could keep the secret no more: the mysterious sausages belonged to 'the Big Fella'.

The next few days were nerve-racking. Suppose the Tans called and raided the larder? Would we crack under pressure? The whole family was warned by my father not to talk about the sausages. A couple of days passed. Batty was due to collect the parcel the next morning at six o'clock, and we were looking forward to the end of our ordeal. However, the night before, as I said my prayers at the side of the bed, I heard the familiar sound of the Tan lorries pulling up outside. My father ran upstairs immediately. 'Eoin,' he said, 'go down to the larder, grab the sausages, and hide them under your bed.' I ran downstairs hurriedly, without thinking. I could hear shouting outside and then banging on the door. I seized the sausages, and ran back up to my bedroom. I lifted up the bed, and threw the small parcel on to the bare floorboards underneath. Next I heard an unfamiliar foreign-sounding voice from below. 'Ee-ah, 'oo's ap veah? Cam daan immediately, like.' I crept cautiously downstairs and saw three Tans standing in our kitchen. One of them looked at me accusingly. 'Ooo's vis lihul rascul, ven? Been 'idin' sumfing vat you shouldn't 'av bin idin', uv u, u cheeky lihul blighta? 'Aintcha' goh no respect faw lawrrrrr n' awda?' I replied that I had done nothing wrong, but it was too late. My father had said that it was me who had deliberately hidden the sausages and that he knew nothing about it. I was immediately arrested and taken into custody. Luckily, the Crossley Tender taking me to the barracks was fired on during the journey, and I managed to escape. When I returned, my father said that he had informed on me because it was the first thing that came into his head. I told him that I understood, but it soured the relationship between us for some years afterwards. It was only in the 1950s, when I was instrumental in cutting the old-age pension, thus forcing my father out on the streets for a time, that I was able to gain some retribution.

The next day, a tall, handsome man I had never met before came to collect the sausages. He spoke with a Cork accent and patted me on the head. 'Who's the little patriot?' he said. I replied that I didn't know. He gave me a sixpenny bit and told me to buy as many sweets as I liked. I said that I wouldn't be able to buy as many sweets as I liked for sixpence; could he give me fifty pounds instead? He laughed, then jinked out the door with a curiously lithe action which I later came to recognize as a mark of effeminacy. (Michael Mac-Liammoir, the notorious homosexual who ran the Gate Theatre for many years, made a similar motion when leaving a room; halfway between a leap and a skip.) As the stranger stood in the doorway, he paused for a moment, looked me straight in the eye, and said, 'I'm Collins.' Then he disappeared into the Dublin fog. Despite the fact that he reappeared twenty minutes later to ask (rather self-consciously, I remember) for more detailed directions to find his way back into town, I felt that I had met a truly heroic figure.

The stories of Collins's many escapes from the Black and Tans and the Auxiliaries (an equally notorious bunch of cunts) are legendary. One time, with the help of the Lord Mayor of Cork, Tomas MacCurtain, he was placed in a bag and flushed down a toilet to escape detection; on another occasion he posed as Lloyd George when he was stopped by some Auxies on O'Connell Street. This foolhardy act of defiance, pretending to be the British Prime Minister whilst carrying the burden of being the most wanted man in the Empire on his shoulders, was typical of Collins's bravado. Legends grew up around him; people became overexcited and illogical when describing his feats. Men would have sexual erections at the mere mention of his name, just as if they were thinking about a naked girl. Some of these stories were decidedly fanciful, yet it was claimed that they were

true. I myself have heard it said that he could become invisible at the drop of a hat; that he could make a dropped hat become invisible; that he could disappear into thin air; or that he could stand completely still, without even blinking, for months at a time. (This talent had come in very useful when he had posed as a statue outside the RIC barracks in Clonmel for three weeks after a daring raid for arms.) A popular rumour at the time had it that he even played the trombone solo on 'The Man From Clonakilty' by Sean Sloane and the Mexicans, a popular gramophone record of the time. It was often hard to separate fact from fiction when it came to Collins, which is why most people didn't bother.

1922, the year in which I reached the age of ten, was also the year of the split over the Anglo-Irish Treaty, which had been signed at the end of the previous year, 1921. As I have mentioned, my parents disagreed with Collins over its proposals (in his words 'the freedom to achieve freedom . . . and then maybe a bit more freedom . . . and then . . . who knows . . . a bit more again?'). They took de Valera's side in the subsequent civil war which ended in a defeat for the anti-Treatyites. It was a sad time for the country, which was greatly divided on the issue. From my own memory, I recall that men with beards and dark hair tended to support Collins, while girls, fair-headed men, children, short people, women nearing retirement age who worked in the catering industry, and shepherds (?!) tended to go along with Dev. My father took no part in the fighting himself. He was appalled at the bloodshed, and preferred to stay at home making endless cups of strong, sugary tea and reading of the daily atrocities which, by the beginning of 1923, were listed in *The Irish Independent* in a 'one to ten' order, rather like the pop charts of today. Here is a typical list of 'outrages' from January of that year:

1. Headless corpse found in ditch near Cahirciveen with a note pinned to his coat reading 'No Heads for Traitors!'
2. Free State troops surround and blow up a badger set in Clones.
3. Irregular concert party performing a musical comedy in Mullingar jeered at by passing acolyte of the late Sinn Fein president Arthur Griffith.
4. Knees and ankles of unidentified Free State officer found in a bag buried under a tree near Monastrevin.
5. Head found in ditch near Ennis with a note pinned to its ear reading 'No Bodies for Traitors!'
6. Photograph of Eamon de Valera urinated on by second-year students at St Patrick's seminary, Co. Limerick.
7. Pro-Free State provost of St Patrick's kidnapped and forced to perform an exotic dance for the amusement of unknown men as retaliation for incident above.
8. Hens tarred and feathered by drunken Free State troops near Macroom.
9. Cattle stampeded through 'Miss Claremorris' beauty pageant by men shouting out 'Up the Republic!'
10. Hens de-feathered and original feathers reattached by Republican sympathizers (see original incident, no. 8, above).

During that bitter and bloody summer of 1922 I remember going on long walks with my father in the Dublin mountains where we talked endlessly about the struggle for national liberation. His great regard for previous generations who had suffered in earlier times was always evident on these walks. As we passed various hedges, he would often look at them closely, and after some consideration say, 'Ah, yes, that would have been a hedge where there was a school.' Of course, stories of 'hedge schools' were familiar to all nationalist children, although the idea that a hedge could be a school seemed a strange idea to me at the time, and I asked my father to elaborate. I remember our conversation went something like this:

'You see, Eoin, in the old days, the British forbade the Catholic people of Ireland to have any education. But the priests used to gather their flock together in hedges and teach them there.'

'Daddy, why did they have to meet in hedges? Could the priest not have taught the people at the side of the road?'

'No. The school had to be in a hedge.'

'So, they're all in a hedge? All the people with the priest teaching them?'

'Yes.'

'But you can't actually get into a hedge.'

'No ... but there's probably a bit at the side of the hedge where they might be all able to fit in. Technically they'd probably be "under" the hedge rather than "in" it.'

'It'd be very hard to see in a hedge, Daddy. Especially if you were at the back.'

'That's right, Eoin. Practically one of the worst places you could go to school would be in a hedge.'

'Did they have classes up trees?'

'They might have had the odd one or two, say, for instance, if the British had burnt the hedges. But generally, they'd look around for another hedge, and get into that one. Isn't it a terrible thing to think that the British hated the Irish so much that they prodded them with hot pokers featuring pornographic drawings of the Pope* and forced them to go to school in a hedge? What were they thinking of at all, at all?'

When I remember those far-off days, I think often of the great men of the time; heroes such as the Flying Column commander Sean Hales in Cork, or Liam Lynch the uncompromising Republican hard man from Limerick. I particularly think of patriots like Hales and Lynch while soaring high over the Irish sea on a jet bound to or from Heathrow (I still make occasional visits to London for the odd conference or two). There I am, thousands of feet up in the air, sipping a 7-Up and struggling to open a small packet of 'cocktail biscuits' in a silver foil packet with my ninety-year-old fingers. The silver foil proves to be as impenetrable as Fort Knox, and I soon stop trying to gain entry. Instead I look down at the vast sea below and think of our Republican past. Often, I pick up the in-flight magazine to have a

* There is no hard evidence to substantiate this particular claim of my father's.

bit of a browse. This is a journal very much determined to show off the 'new Ireland' to foreign visitors. Forget about Church domination and farmyard animals wandering about the house; that's all in the past. No, no; instead we are presented with motoring columns, interviews with Irish poets unheard of in their own country but discussed by academics in the canteen of Ohio University, and the 'new generation of Irish chefs'. Typically, I will come across a fawning four-page profile of one of these ludicrous gastronomes. 'Hugely successful', he is just about to open his fifteenth seafood emporium which will serve the most delicious grilled and buttered shark in the Western Hemisphere. And he is still not thirty years old! As I read about his views on 'simple cooking' and the fifty-eight different ways one can sauté a potato, I think of Liam Lynch and Sean Hales. During the civil war, they became enemies, but were both heartbroken by the conflict that engulfed men who had a short while earlier been comrades in arms. As they pondered the true meaning of 'Pearse's Republic' and the best way to achieve it, would their thoughts, however briefly, ever have jumped forward eighty years to contemplate 'the new generation of Irish chefs'? To paraphrase some of the newer Irish contemporary playwrights and novelists 'bollocks they would'. I think it was a stroke of great luck for both men that they were brutally killed during the civil war and did not live to see the country the way it is today.

At the time of the terrible troubles, I was still a child, and largely unconcerned with such matters. My battlefield was the playground. My ambush was the games I played with the other schoolchildren. My bridge blowing-up was the teaching I received. My being stopped at improvised checkpoints by men with long grey coats and flat caps was the margin at the side of my copybooks.

I was not a great student at this early age, and preferred the excitements of the playground to the drudgery of schooling. During break times, myself and the other children would play football with pieces of paper (we were rather naive and didn't know we were supposed to roll them up into a ball) as well as other games such as 'running around' and 'chasing'.

Up until twelve years of age, I was educated by nuns of the Brigidine Order. But in the year 1924 the responsibility for my schooling was placed into the sure and capable hands of the Christian Brothers.

CHAPTER 2

The Awakening Lamp

'Hello there! Welcome to St Fintan's!'

Brother Euclid Crowe gripped my hand firmly and shook it frantically for what seemed like an age. I had just passed through the gates of St Fintan's Christian Brothers School in Rathfarnham for the very first time. The unusually tall Brother Crowe, who absolutely towered over me, was almost gibbering with excitement. I soon found out from some of the older boys that this was his normal reaction on the first day back at school, such was his exhilaration at meeting new pupils. Even when he was talking to me, his attention suddenly wandered to another boy standing some distance away who was looking around at his new surroundings with some trepidation. 'Look at that fella; he's a lovely looking blondey chap. I'll just go over and have a word with him. God, he's *gorgeous!*' He left and quickly introduced himself to the other new boy, whose hand was soon enmeshed in the vice-like grip that mine had been in a few moments earlier.

After a couple of days at Fintan's, I discovered that Brother Crowe was nicknamed 'The Rooster'. This was not only because he used to holler excitedly, but also for the reason that he looked rather like a hen, due mostly to his alarmingly feathery skin, a common characteristic of many Brothers. I liked Brother Crowe immediately (despite the fact that he'd almost crushed my hand!) and was delighted when I discovered that he was to be my Irish teacher. Thanks to my mother's great enthusiasm for the native tongue, I was already a 'convert to the cause', and The Rooster's tuition was something I embraced wholeheartedly. During my years in St Fintan's he was someone I always looked up to (I had to; he was almost seven feet tall!).

Around this time I made it a lifelong resolution to learn a new word of Irish every day, and it was only two weeks ago when I finally 'ran out'. I have since made up my own Irish words for things: for example, 'Gna Na Goicompuitoir' (Computer Porn), and 'Rug Ti Gnaiste' (lesbianism). It is interesting that there are no words in the Irish language for the more base experiments in sexuality. It proves to me that the Irish race is an essentially pure breed, and that the horrific onslaught of liberalism from England and America is essentially alien to us. What a shame this fundamental truth is not reflected in our national television stations.

My time at St Fintan's was a happy period in my life. The Brothers believed in firm discipline, and while this could be occasionally painful – physical manifestations included being beaten with leathers, kicked unconscious and spat at – no boy who 'played by the rules' had much to fear. There was only one death in my time in Fintan's, and the issue was so clear-cut that it was deemed unnecessary even to hold an inquiry. The idea of an organization such as Amnesty International would have been regarded as ludicrous in those days. You had to be able to 'take it', and if you couldn't, there was no one to run off to (unlike now).* A Brother once stood on my head for an hour while I recited the decades of the rosary in Latin. I admit it was unpleasant at the time, but if he hadn't done it, how would I have turned out? Like Boyzone or the Corrs?

One day, as I was playing football in the schoolyard, I saw a boy, a few years older than me, reading a catechism beside the toilets. (I call them toilets, but they were little more than cisterns with flushing devices connected to porcelain bowls.) He had jet-black, sticking-up hair, and seemed to have more freckles on his face than there were border patrols in border-patrol areas. I was intrigued by the fact that he was reading a catechism rather than playing football – although he later claimed that he could read a catechism and play football at the same time.† After our little match was over, I made my way over to him. I introduced myself, and he told me that his name was Gloinn McTire. It was the beginning of a lifelong friendship that has lasted for ages. I asked him why he was not playing football – did he not like games? He replied that, yes, he liked games, but that he preferred reading about spiritual matters. I immediately knew that he shared my deep religious faith, and it has been a bond that has kept us close for almost a hundred

* Amnesty International.
† A skill he shares with Pope John Paul (II).

years. Gloinn was fifteen years old at this time, three years senior to me, and he would inevitably win our regular nude-wrestling matches, refereed by a similarly starkers Brother Crowe ('Yez have to be nude, lads; there'll be less friction'). I soon discovered that my new friend had a quick sense of humour, and enjoyed ribbing me about my stammer, lisp and crossed eyes. He told me that his parents came from Kerry and were both committed (literally; they'd both been declared insane and sent to a secure prison) nationalists. Something that Gloinn and I were to share over the years was our unswerving conviction (literally; we have both been convicted on arms offences) in a thirty-two county Protestant-free Catholic Republic. He lived not far from me – by this time my family had moved to Harold's Cross – and we often discussed religion and the national question on our way home from school. (I say 'discussed', but we really just talked about how great it was to be an Irish Catholic in the 1920s.) Gloinn also had a fanatical love of the native language, and suggested that I accompany him the next summer to the Gaeltacht, the Irish-speaking region of Connacht, where he would be attending St Fionn's College. Needless to say, when I told my parents about this invitation, they were delighted, and encouraged me in my new friendship. That summer of 1925 would live long in my memory.

We left on the 6th of June (Gloinn's birthday), a glorious day of sunshine and gentle mists. The mists were so gentle that one could actually blow them into fields, and I had great fun demonstrating this to Gloinn.

I remember clearly walking to the train station at Kingsbridge, dragging our two large, bulky suitcases behind me (as I was the youngest, I had to drag both of them). A strap had broken on one, and it was an almighty struggle to keep the whole thing from falling apart. Luckily, we found a compartment on the train which we had completely to ourselves, until a rather arrogant-looking gentleman got on at Athenry. I took an immediate dislike to this character, and I could see that Gloinn also seemed disturbed by his presence. The man had a full, untrimmed beard, which was unusual for the time, and by his haughty manner and unfriendliness, I began to suspect that he was a Protestant, though I had never actually come across one before. When he behaved in a petulant way with the ticket inspector, asking how far Galway was and inquiring if the window in the compartment could be closed, my suspicions were confirmed. He also spoke with a snooty English accent and when we heard an angelus bell sound at 6 o'clock, he failed to turn away from his newspaper, *The 'Irish' Times* (another clue – *The 'Irish' Times* was, and remains, a notoriously pro-Protestant paper). At this point, myself and Gloinn started praying loudly so that the man would know he was in the presence of two committed Gaels. Afterwards, on our trip by pony and trap to Clifden, Gloinn and I talked about Protestantism, and its malignant influence on Irish life. I remember this discussion being a fiery one as we debated the various contentious points. Gloinn's parents had taken a moderate line on the subject, pointing out that many Irish nationalists, such as Robert

Emmet, Wolfe Tone, and more recently Ernest Blythe (who I was to meet much later in life) were Protestants, but they still agreed that at the end of the day, they were all going to hell. My parents, however, had taught me that to be a Protestant was to be in league with the very devil itself, and always to bless myself and cross the street if I came upon one. (My father would always have a bath, complete with lemon-scented disinfectant, if he suspected that he had seen a 'Prod' at first hand.) Merely thinking about them gave me the shivers, and despite the liveliness of our debate, it was with some relief when the Irish college came into view. There would be no Prods at St Fionn's!

In 1962, I produced a pamphlet for schools entitled 'The Protestant Mind'. It is a subject that has fascinated me for most of my adult life. When one sees figures such as 'The Reverend' Ian Paisley or that archetypal 'Man of Ulster' John Taylor of the Official Unionists, what traditional Catholic has not thought to himself 'I wonder what makes a mind like that tick?' So, what would we find if we were to slice open the head of John Taylor? (as the IRA attempted in 1972!) We would see a mind that, cosmetically, does not look that much different to a Catholic one. Yet there *are* differences. The Protestant mind is of course meticulous. It is ideally suited to tackle mathematical problems and algebraic puzzles. Many of the great nuclear physicists, such as Albert Einstein, have been Protestants. The Protestant mind loves tackling problems and finding solutions. It loves logic. It loves black. It loves white. It has not much time for grey.

It does not like to rush to a solution, but will take its time to ponder; to weigh up alternatives; to come to a logical conclusion. But of course, there is more to life than mathematics. The Protestant mind is confused by the spiritual world. When confronted with the illogicality of Christianity, it metaphorically – and sometimes even literally – explodes. When it cannot comprehend the goodness and grace of the One True Faith of Catholicism, it takes refuge in the structural simplicity of Protestantism. The mind that might easily spend several hours on a train journey pondering a crossword in *The Irish Times* would be disturbed and disorientated by the notion that contraception is wrong.

Sadly, my educational pamphlet was not widely distributed in schools. It was judged to be, according to a (Protestant) official in the Department of Education who took offence at it, 'as inherently fascistic as eliminationist anti-Semitism'. In my experience, when people take offence at something, it is invariably because they know that there is a large grain of truth in what has offended them. Otherwise, why would they complain about it? This is what undoubtedly happened in the case of my pamphlet.

I admit to a certain loneliness at St Fionn's in my first weeks there, but soon my homesickness was replaced by a genuine, almost insane, love for my teachers and fellow pupils, as well as the beautiful scenery of the West, which I have subsequently adored all my life.

After lessons, in the unusually sunny and warm weather, we would skip gaily – almost haphazardly – along the roads, go swimming in the local lakes and fish in the streams. I must admit, I had little luck fishing, and often returned to my dormitory early for further study. Once, Gloinn informed me that he had caught a few tiddlers, and I thought for some years afterwards that he had contracted a sexual disease from a girl in the college. As I have mentioned, ignorance about such things was the norm in those days, and I suspect it made for a happier and less confusing time for everybody. I was certainly aware of girls, and their reputation for leading boys astray, but my interests at thirteen years old lay elsewhere (unlike nowadays, when I would be doubtless 'jacking off' to pornographic images on the Internet). It would still be some years before I met my dear late wife, Noreen, whose sexual tastes happily matched my own (i.e. complete non-interest).

A very popular pastime in those days in St Fionn's was the very fashionable 'sing-song'. I remember many nights spent by the fire singing away with the other students to our hearts' content. All over Ireland, people at the time would often break into a melody to either cheer themselves up or just to break the monotony of day-to-day life. I recall with fondness many evenings at home when neighbours would come round for a 'sing-song' which could often last well into the night. Unlike today, most people in the country knew up to sixty or seventy songs, and when one person in a bar or in a house started up a tune, he could be certain that everybody else in the room would soon join in. A 'sing-song' could be a great tonic if one found oneself in a depressing or dangerous situation. I remember once

walking with my father near a section of the river Slaney in Wexford, when we heard the sound of people singing nearby. The noise gradually grew louder, and my father looked around to see where it was coming from. He was more than surprised to see about four people clinging on to a tree trunk as they headed towards a very steep and hazardous waterfall. 'Listen to that, Eoin,' said my father. 'Those people are having a great old sing-song!' It was obvious that they had little chance of survival, but I could still hear them singing as they slipped over the edge of the waterfall and hurtled to their deaths. They had obviously decided that although they were about to perish, and there was absolutely no prospect of rescue, spirits could be best kept up by resorting to a bit of an old tune. There was quite a big piece about the tragedy in the next issue of *The Wexford People*, and my father was able to confirm, along with another man on the opposite river bank, that the unfortunate individuals clinging to the tree went to meet their maker belting out a stirring rendition of 'The Croppy Boy'. According to the man on the other river bank who was closer to them, 'They sounded in great form!'

My time in the Gaeltacht also led me to the works of Padraig Pearse. Pearse, like me, had loved the area, and felt that it represented the purest and most definitive spirit of Ireland. I began to read his poetry and it inspired me to compose some poems of my own. As I write this now, I am looking at a faded copybook from that time. I suspect it dates from the summer of 1926 (I went to St Fionn's every year up to 1929), and it contains three poems. Another pupil in my class, Denis Gubney, a lovely gentle fellow from Mayo, was also a budding poet, and we used to show each other our work. Needless to say, we were rather tentative and embarrassed about our efforts, but a kind or encouraging word from another enthusiastic novice was always appreciated. Gloinn also dabbled in poetry (and indeed sketching), but prose was always his preferred medium. One of my poems in the copybook is called 'An Colgach Gruaim' ('The Truculent Gloom') and I translate it here from the Irish:

> *The Truculent Gloom*
> *Like a falling wound,*
> *Treading on the fertile slopes*
> *That took the maiden fair.*
>
> *'Tis gone today,*
> *The mournful dawn*
> *Of ships across the bay,*
> *Flailing playfully,*
> *Cry once again*
> *For the Children of Lir.*

I must admit to a certain pride in this poem, as it is remarkably mature for a boy of fourteen. One expects the adolescent mind to produce a sentimental tract that could easily slip into cliché and be devoid of meaning and depth, but this poem falls into neither trap. I often thought of including it in my various books of poetry over the years – it was shortlisted for my 1975 collection *An Rogollach Buachaillearacht* (*The Rollicking Apron*) – but

I felt it too redolent of its time. It never quite fitted into a satisfactory niche for me, and until now has remained unpublished. I may also add that in the Gaelic version it rhymes beautifully.

A sad note about Denis Gubney: after a career in Customs and Excise, in later life he became manager of the Mayside Arms Hotel in Foxford, Co. Mayo. While queueing at a cash machine during a hoteliers' conference in California in 1992, he was buggered and then forced to perform oral sex on a drug-crazed rapper during the Los Angeles riots. It would have been particularly galling for Denis to go through such an experience as he absolutely *hated* anything to do with homosexuality. He never quite recovered from the shock and died of a drink-related disease in 1997.

In between our annual visits to Connemara, myself and Gloinn continued our schooling in St Fintan's where we had acquired the nicknames of 'Arsewipe' and 'Uncle Septimus'. I was never quite sure if these names were given to us out of affection or jealousy, but even today I will call Gloinn 'Uncle Septimus' just to annoy him! (Needless to say, he will respond with an immediate 'What are you saying there, Arsewipe?') Irish and History were the subjects that interested me most at school, and I usually did very well in both. These were also Gloinn's preferred topics for study, and there was a good-natured and not overly serious rivalry between us as to who finished top of our respective classes more often. (I usually did.) We spent so much time in each other's company at this stage that some boys in the school began putting nasty rumours around about us, to the effect that we were 'getting up to things' together. I think, dear reader, you may understand what I'm talking about here.* This hideous activity, that from what I can gather seems to be *de rigueur* in English Protestant schools, is, thank God, absent in Irish Catholic schools; even in ones where they play rugby. The idea of me kissing Gloinn, or even finding him attractive in any way, is so ridiculous that it brings tears of laughter to my eyes. Indeed, the photograph of Gloinn on the back cover of the recent paperback edition of his novel *The Trials of Murty Keogh* would hardly suggest that he is a 'great catch' even for the most desperate of spinsters! (No disrespect to his wife Maire intended.) I am happy to say that my relationship with Mr McT. has never involved, or never will involve – especially as we are now both approaching a hundred years of age – having a bath together.

Unfortunately, my grandfather died in the harsh winter of 1928, an event which saddened me greatly. He had been rather senile for some time, and suffered from numerous debilitating delusions, among them the belief that his thoughts were being controlled by the ghost of the Dublin wit and surgeon Oliver St John Gogarty (paradoxically, at that time still alive). His face, due to the pipe cleaners becoming rusty and old, had also become detached from the rest of his head, giving him a

* Buggery.

ludicrously surreal appearance (he would have made a great subject for the painter Salvador Dali!), while, in yet another freak dynamite explosion, he had lost an ear and part of his thumb. I remember his funeral being a melancholy affair, but the priest comforted us all by reminding us that my grandfather's great faith would lead him to his eternal award. (He may have meant 'reward'. I don't think one receives an award when one enters Heaven, no matter how spiritual a life one has led.) The old man had so few material possessions that he had never bothered to make a will, but he let it be known that if there were any sticks in his house that had been left over from lighting the fire, then I was to have them. A subsequent search through his sad, untidy tenement room uncovered three sticks hidden under a box of erotic photographs featuring Victorian ladies from the 1880s in quaintly suggestive poses. I never burnt the sticks, but have them still.

The summer of 1929 was the last I spent in St Fionn's. On our final day there, the students, under the watchful eye of our master, Mr O'Bruen, gathered at a public house close to the school to celebrate. I had my first taste of porter that day, and found that I didn't like it. As I have mentioned, I have never developed a taste for alcohol of any description, and am proud to say that I have been a lifelong 'teetotaller'. Gloinn admitted to me when we were in the pub in Connemara that he had taken a drink before, and I have a memory of him knocking back a considerable number of pints on that summer day in 1929, to the increasing disapproval of Mr

O'Bruen. In the years afterwards, it all went a bit sour for my old friend, and he would be the first to admit that the power of prayer was often called upon to combat his dependence on the bottle. His faith has been a great source of strength to him over the years, and I myself have lost count of the number of masses I have had said for him. A turning point occurred for Gloinn when he went to a retreat in Wicklow in the late 1940s and met Father Tom Winlick, a legendary figure who had just arrived from Chicago where he had done sterling work with alcoholics. Father Winlick's approach was a very basic one; to tell drunkards to 'cop on to themselves' and pray for relief. His motto was quite simply 'Stop Drinking!', which he would regularly roar out at the top of his voice. He also wore a T-shirt emblazoned with the motto at a time when it was very uncommon to see priests wearing casual clothes of this kind. Father Winlick himself had been a fierce drinker, who, due to his dependence on whiskey, had run up a debt in his parish in Philadelphia of several million dollars. I don't know the exact details of his conversion to abstentionism, but Gloinn told me that it happened after he got knifed in the head while on a typical all-night 'bender' with the legendary and colourful confidant to Al Capone and 'chaplain to the mob' Father Huey Morocco. Thankfully, after his encounter with Father Winlick, Gloinn's drinking became less of a problem for a while. But he has never given it up entirely, as he claims it is something he enjoys a great deal and helps him to relax. Even today, at over ninety years of age, he will still get wildly, madly drunk to the point of caricature. When I have seen him at a low ebb, such as the time he drank the oil from a lamp in St Benedict's Cathedral in Lausanne, I have often thought 'there but for the grace of God, that's me'.

I left St Fintan's for the last time in the summer of 1930. I was unclear in my mind as to what I wanted to do when I left school and had sought advice from the Brothers there. I must admit that at that time, I did consider answering the call of the religious life, and I had a long discussion with The Rooster about this, conducted in his bed on a lazy summer afternoon just before my final exams. He gently rubbed the back of my leg and stressed to me the importance of having a vocation. It was not something that one should stumble into, as dedicating one's life to God is a big commitment, both for oneself and for God. I asked him how I would know if I had a genuine calling. He said that he had got his one day while he was out in the cowshed at his parents' farm in Westmeath. He'd felt dizzy, and had gone to bed for the afternoon. When he'd woken up, he'd felt like becoming a Christian Brother. He asked me if I'd ever had that type of feeling, and I had to admit in all honesty that I hadn't. The Rooster said that in that case, I shouldn't bother with it, and anyway, the money wasn't great. I realized that my future would lie outside the priesthood.

A very funny incident once happened to me in America, concerning the similarities of the words 'vocation' and

'vacation'. I was chatting to my cousin Eileen's son Sean, a lovely fellow who at that time (the early 1970s) was just about to leave high school (the American version of second-ary school). Eileen is a very devout Catholic, and Sean, her only son, was seriously considering joining the priesthood. 'What should I do, Uncle Eoin?' he asked me. I said that it was very important for him to be sure he had a vocation. He looked at me with a bemused look on his face. 'Why would I go away to enjoy myself at a time like this?' he asked in all sincerity. We were both very puzzled by this misunderstanding, until I explained what a vocation was. He thought I was talking about a holiday!! It was definitely one of the greatest laughs I think I've ever had.

I also discussed my potential career with my mother. (I was still on bad terms with my father after he'd shopped me to the Tans in 1920.) During our conversation, she mentioned that she knew a man in the Department of the Irish Language (the Irish-language department which dealt mostly with matters concerning the Irish language), and would I consider a position there? The more I thought about it, the more it appealed to me. It would be a steady job which would eventually offer a pension of a pound a week in fifty years' time, so that even if I didn't enjoy it, I could still look forward to a secure retirement. However, since I loved the native tongue so much, I was certain that I would have a rewarding time there. A couple of days afterwards, I met the man from the department, a small, balding, quiet individual called Pol O'Flick, and he said that I would have to take some entrance exams. These I subsequently completed, and did well enough to be admitted to the department. I began my first day there on September 13th, 1930, a date I've always remembered because I made a note of it in my diary at the time. I was to spend eight happy years in the Department of Irish, during which I would marry, and my son Lorcan would be born for the first time.

CHAPTER 3

Gorillas in the Mist

Mr O'Flick was my immediate superior when I started in the department, and I couldn't have asked for a nicer man to work under. We spoke Irish *all* the time, and I learnt even more words and phrases from him. (Later he would be the first man to translate 'Third Reich' into the Gaelic.) I remember he had very hairy ears (not hair growing out from the ear, but an actual thin layer of fluff stretching from the lobe right around the rim.* This embarrassed him somewhat, and his nickname in the department was 'Gnog Ailleachaille' ('Ear Muffs'). We both used to attend 7 o'clock mass in Earlsfort Terrace every morning before going to work, and I once heard him yell out in despair for relief from the constant persecution and mockery. One unpleasant individual who worked with us for some months during a temporary transfer from another department was merciless in his torment of Mr O'Flick. 'You hairy-eared bastard', 'you bugger with the hairy ears on you' and the even more wounding 'O'Flick, you f**k face, hairy-eared monster' were some of the milder forms of abuse that the poor man was subjected to. We all breathed a sigh of relief

---

* The rim of the ear, as opposed to the rim of the anus.

when this individual's time in our department came to an end.

Mr O'Flick lived in a charming cottage in Ringsend, and I would often go there for tea. In later years I was usually accompanied by my fiancée, Noreen. He was a widower who lived alone, but his cottage was so tidy that I'm sure he occasionally got a woman (or an unusually tidy, and probably 'camp', man!) in to clean it. One day, he quite casually mentioned that he had known Padraig Pearse quite well, and I badgered him with questions about my hero until he got sick of it and left. Another interesting fact about Mr O'Flick (I never called him Pol) was that one leg was markedly shorter than the other. However, he compensated for this by always walking with his left leg on the road and his right leg on the pavement, a perambulatory 'arse-over-tit' style, which resembled the motion of those gravity-driven plastic 'action-walking' figures that were given away free with packets of cornflakes some years ago.

A disturbing trend amongst modern revisionist historians is to portray Padraig Pearse as a homosexual, just because he never had any girlfriends and wrote poems about being in love with young boys. This is like saying that someone who goes into a shop, holds up the shopkeeper and takes money from the till, is a thief. There is no proof at all (apart from sworn statements from witnesses) that Pearse indulged in unusual sexual acts. Such was his single-minded determination to die for Ireland under the bloodiest possible circum-

stances that I doubt if he ever had any thoughts about sex at all.

It is almost impossible to imagine Pearse's penis in the process of erection, but at a summer school in Sligo, which I attended a couple of years ago, a revisionist historian actually suggested this scenario, and even presented a slide show to illustrate his point. It was a very crude and unnecessary visual display which sickened all who saw it. The memory of Pearse was sullied by the presentation and it seems that the once unquestioned acceptance of his greatness as a scholar, poet and leader of the Irish people is now constantly under threat.

My work in the department was mainly translating many of the governmental files left over from the English administration into Irish. One day, while I was at my desk, the poet W. B. Yeats wandered in. I must admit that I was never a fan of Yeats's rather 'high falutin'' poems. They seemed to be written from a very Protestant perspective, and were very intellectual and pretentious. Yeats looked like a woman in his big cloak, and I thought there was a smell of sickly sweet perfume coming from him. I found this was often a common characteristic in a Protestant. Our meeting was brief. He made some remark about swans, then asked where the toilet was. I told him where to find it, and he left. No doubt, even while he was asking me where the toilet was, he was thinking about how superior he was to me, just because I was a Catholic.

A regular part of the job involved an annual visit to Donegal, which I always greatly enjoyed. I usually stayed with a wonderful man called Michael Judge, then aged around seventy-five, a very tall, white-haired character who had been an early member of the Gaelic League and some years later went on to contribute the regular bridge column to *An Phoblacht*, the IRA's official newspaper. His cottage in Gweedore was made completely out of turf. This puzzled me, as a turf fire also burned constantly in the grate, and I could never understand why the entire cottage didn't catch fire. One day, on my second or third visit to Donegal, Michael, completely out of the blue, sat me down in a chair beside the fire and looked me straight in the eye. 'Are you ready?' he asked. I didn't quite know what he meant, but I answered tentatively in the affirmative. 'Right, so. Let's go!' Michael then proceeded to explain to me, in an admirably cool and calm fashion, the facts of life.

Needless to say, I was both frightened and appalled by some of the things he came out with, but he never panicked, and got the whole thing over with in as quick and as businesslike a way as possible. 'What do you think of that?' he asked me when he'd finished. 'Do you like the sound of it? How would you like doing that type of thing? You look like the kind of young fellow who loves sex.' (He could hardly have been more wrong!) The old man seemed very keen to get my thoughts on the subject, but I was rather shell-shocked at that stage and didn't know how to respond. He talked with me about anal sex (?) [*author's question mark, brackets and italics*] for a long time, often going into needlessly (I thought) detailed descriptions of drawings he'd seen in a library in London depicting the act. I had to agree with him that the whole area of sex is a bit of a 'hornets' nest' and that one needs steady nerves when dealing with it. Michael's attitude to his own sexuality always both puzzled and amused me. He once told me, with a wicked smile, that he had circumcised himself with a penknife 'to see what the thing would look like' ('Horrible!'). He never married, remaining a bachelor all his long life, but enjoyed explaining the facts of life to young fellows from Dublin when they stayed with him in his cottage. I saw him once, in the kitchen, standing naked in front of his full-length mirror (which he had found in a local bog), deep in thought, carefully studying his own reflection. At intervals, he would pinch and manipulate parts of his wizened flesh with his long fingers, in a state of quiet, studied fascination. When he finished this ritual, he knelt down, said three Hail Marys and then recited the words of the 1916 Proclamation of Independence. What was going through the mind of the old Gaelic Leaguer, I wondered.

Armed with new-found knowledge of the facts of life, earning a regular income, and blessed with good health, my mind turned to thoughts of marriage. I used to regularly attend dances at the old St Benignus Hall, which was located on Capel Street, until I realized it was an all-male dancing club, so I then went to the Marmelite Hall in Sandyford for their regular Saturday night sessions. After several months of rejection by women who, with the benefit of hindsight, I now realize were probably lesbians, I was about to give up all hope of ever finding anyone to dance with me. But then my luck suddenly changed. One night I was sipping a glass of milk at the bar (these were the days before 7-Up!) when I noticed a pretty (or so I thought at the time), dark-haired girl sitting at a table by the dance floor. I wondered why she wasn't dancing, and speculated that it might be because she had a 'clubbed' foot. However, when she stood up to come over to the bar, I could see that there was nothing wrong with her. I could hardly believe my good fortune when she arrived beside me to order some drinks from the barman. It was unusual for a girl to order drinks in those days unless she was a whore, but I could see plainly that this girl had never accepted money for sex. I was rather shy with the ladies at the time and must admit that I didn't know much about the 'fairer sex' (not that I know much more now!) but I was determined to ask this delightful creature for a dance. I prayed that she wouldn't notice my stammer, lisp or crossed eyes, and popped the question. To my great relief, she agreed to my request, and after returning the drinks to her table – she had come with a rather plain-looking, very small friend – we took to the dance floor. I asked her name, and she said that it was Noreen Harte, and she was from Naas 'in the county of Kildare'. We had a grand time that evening, and we made plans to see each other again.

I saw a lot of Noreen over the next few months, and found out more about her. Often she would be accompanied by her small, plain-looking friend who I discovered was called Mona. Noreen and Mona remained great pals throughout the years, and Mona is still alive today. On account of her unremarkable looks, Gloinn used to say that she was 'more like Bord Na Mona [the Irish semi-state company which extracts turf from bogs] than the Mona Lisa!' This was a very funny remark, and I always used to 'crack up' when my old friend would come out with it. Once, Mona and Gloinn's equally unattractive spouse Maire got into a vicious fist fight in Gloinn's house. It happened as a result of an argument they had after Mona had gone to buy a bag of chips and had returned without tomato ketchup which Maire had asked her to generously pour over her portion. This 'Clash of the Uglies' (as Gloinn referred to it) was a very unpleasant spectacle indeed. It had wider repercussions for Mona as well, as she received a blow to the womb during the encounter and had to be hospitalized. She was subsequently unable to have babies.

To my delight, I discovered that Noreen shared my interest in the Irish language and the national issue. She was also a devout Catholic and, like myself, a daily communicant. Her parents were ignorant farming people and, as was usual amongst most girls in Ireland at the time, she had come to Dublin to train as a nurse. When I met her, she was living in a flat in Fairview with her aunt.

A very funny incident happened the first time I took Noreen to meet Gloinn. I was very keen for his approval, and

wanted 'the new girl' to make a good impression. To this end, I bought her a dress in a shop in Grafton Street. I must say, I did not know much about women's fashion in those days (not that I know much more now!) and I asked the sales assistant to select the garment for me. This she did, settling almost at once on a fetching green number. I was more than happy with her choice (especially since she'd chosen the national colour!) and, after I paid her, she packed the dress neatly in a box and handed it to me to take home. I thought nothing more of it, but lo and behold, when the time came for Noreen to try it on, she discovered it was too big! I had forgotten to tell the sales assistant what size Noreen was! To be honest, I didn't even know that women came in different sizes. In the end, Noreen wore one of her own dresses, Gloinn thought she was wonderful, and the evening went very well. But the story of the green dress was told in our house many times over the years, and I honestly think it's one of the funniest things that ever happened to me.

> *Faith of Your Legions Strong,*
> *Till Come the Judgement Day.*
> *O Glorious Eireann, what's that din?*
> *'Tis People Come to Pray.*

The beautiful hymn above was one of many sung at the Eucharistic Congress in Dublin in 1932, one of the best things I've ever been at. This annual event usually took place every couple of years (like a kind of spiritual World Cup) and it was a great honour for Ireland to host the festivities. All the 'big guns' of the Catholic Church were in attendance except 'the man himself', the Holy Father, who would not come amongst us until many years later. (The visit of Pope John Paul (II) in 1979 would be an event organized to a great degree by myself and Gloinn.) During the Congress I would also have the honour of meeting for the first time the Primate of all Ireland, His Eminence, Cardinal Joseph MacRory, with whom I subsequently became firm friends.

Preparations for the event had begun some years before with the launch of a Crusade of Prayer for the success of the Congress. Three quarters of a million prayer leaflets had been dispatched to all corners of Ireland, and the figures quoted in the Congress handbook show the devotion to the Church that the people had at the time. The list of good works promised up to the end of October 1930 read as follows:

Masses – 2,549,931

Holy Communions – 1,926,166

Stations of the Cross – 390,752

Visits to Blessed Sacrament – 2,026,128

Little Office of the Blessed Virgin Mary – 463,465 ? [*author's question mark*]

Acts of Self-Denial – 4,270,795

Other Spiritual Acts – 10,024,590

My own efforts are included in every category in the statistics above (except for Little Office of the Virgin Mary, as I never knew what that actually was). For example, I completed seventy-three acts of self-denial by June 1932, including fasting to the point of near starvation and wearing unironed trousers, which caused me to be censured by Mr O'Flick at the department until I explained that my action was prompted by religious devotion. (It's a good job I wasn't yet married to Noreen. She would almost have preferred my eternal damnation to the sight of a crinkled trouser leg!) I remember having a disagreement with Gloinn at the time about one of his proposed acts of self-denial. He intended removing the brakes from his bicycle for a period of three months. I differed with him on whether this was within the spirit of the meaning of the term, and whilst concurring that this measure would certainly put his life in grave danger, thus gaining him some hard won 'spiritual points', I still thought it did not fit the definition of 'self-denial'. Gloinn argued simply that he was denying himself brakes. In the end, we agreed that his action could happily fit into the category of 'Other Spiritual Acts'. (Thankfully, he never crashed his bicycle during the three-month period. Gloinn agrees with me that God may have been looking after him in this respect. Once He had seen that the initial commitment by Gloinn to put his life in danger had been made, it would have been cruel indeed for the Almighty to 'cash in His chips'.)

Myself, Gloinn and Noreen attended all four days of the Congress in June. The simple, unswerving loyalty of the Irish people to the great faith of St Patrick moved me tremendously, and had the effect of strengthening my Catholicism even further, something I would have believed impossible. I remember on the Saturday evening of the Congress eating a jam sandwich after going to confession and thinking 'this is it'. I suppose the feeling would be similar to the 'high' a paedophile experiences after accessing a particularly juicy web site on the Internet featuring youngsters in various stages of undress.

Let me take you back now to a Sunday in that summer of 1932, the day of the great outdoor mass. It was gloriously sunny, after showers earlier in the morning, and thousands of people had gathered in the wet grass of the open field. I came across my cousin, Louise Daly, at around noon. She had come up from Thurles with her two daughters, Catriona and Anne, leaving her husband Michael to look after the farm. 'He had so wanted to be here, and was quite freaked out [annoyed] that he couldn't make it,' Louise told me. However, he had made the best of things and compensated by decking out the cows at home in the papal colours. They were obviously a family who loved colourful displays of this kind, because I remember Louise's children also wore ribbons in their hair of green, white and orange, while Louise herself had painted a large red cross on her face. (Nowadays one might mistake her for a supporter of the Norwegian soccer team, although of course, personality wise, it would be hard to imagine anyone less inclined to follow Norwegian soccer.) She said that it had been a very troublesome excursion up from the country the previous day, and that all the trains were packed. Anne had lost a 'fun' cardboard cut-out of Pope Pius, which had been given away free with the *Irish Independent*, and they had had to go back to the carriage to look for it.

But the difficulties of their journey had all been worthwhile in the end, and they had never seen so many people gathered in the one spot before. (I think the population density in Tipperary at the time was something like half a person per ten square miles, as 95 per cent of the people had emigrated, died of starvation, been burnt as witches or merely disappeared during the previous century.) As I was chatting to Louise, a man who looked about sixty years of age (I discovered later that he was actually only thirty-nine) approached us and asked if we would care for a bite of his sandwich. I declined, but Louise took a small mouthful after she checked her watch to make sure that she wouldn't be breaking her fast before communion. While she was thanking the stranger, she was distracted by little Catriona pulling at her skirt who said she needed to go to the toilet. Farewells were hurriedly exchanged and Louise and the children took their leave. I continued talking to the man for some time and slowly began to realize that I was in the presence of someone truly spiritual. He had a charisma that somehow reminded me of Rudolf Valentino, although physically he looked almost exactly the complete opposite of the Hollywood star. My companion had broken teeth, greasy thinning grey hair swept over his pockmarked head and wore a suit which seemed to be made out of sackcloth. During our conversation he also kept a very firm grip on one of the belt loops on his trousers in order to stop them falling down. (He explained to me later that he usually had a length of twine which he used as a belt, but this had been stolen when he'd taken his trousers off to go to the toilet in a nearby field.) He told me that his name was Larry Hoey, and that he was the editor of a magazine called *The Glorious Oak* (later re-titled *The Big Oak* after Larry received a letter from the Forestry Commission informing him that *The Glorious Oak* was also the title of their quarterly newsletter). He said that he worked with the poor in Dublin and had recently given up his job in the corporation to concentrate on his religious activities. Later, after mass, I took him to meet Gloinn and he showed us a copy of his magazine. There were many fascinating articles inside, most of which Larry had written himself. For instance, he had done an in-depth report about gramophones which pointed out that most gramophone- and record-shop owners actively contributed money to anti-Catholic organizations. ('No surprises there,' remarked Gloinn resignedly.) Another piece warned of the dangers of Communism, which enraged Gloinn so much he leapt into the air, punching his fist. I remember a memorable (and very funny!) feature about the importance of prayer in marriage, and there was a lively crossword puzzle, also compiled by Larry. 'You don't have to be a Catholic to do the crossword,' Larry claimed, 'but it will certainly help if you are.' Later on, he introduced us to Cardinal MacRory, who turned out to be a stern but charming individual. The Cardinal surprised myself and Gloinn by claiming to be a big Al Jolson fan; at one stage even breaking into a snatch of 'Mammy'. While chatting to His Eminence, I noticed for the first time Larry's tendency to lapse into prayer during an otherwise normal conversation. It was a habit I often recognized during the following years. For instance, if he was talking about buying a loaf of bread, he might say something like, 'I went into a shop Holy Mary Mother of God pray for us sinners now and at the hour of our death to buy a loaf of bread.' He believed that there was no 'proper' time for prayer, and it was an insult to Our Lord to delegate specific times for the activity.

A few weeks after the Congress, still full of Catholic zeal, and with the stirring words of the Papal Nuncio, Dr Alibrandi, ringing in his ears, Gloinn asked Larry if we could contribute articles to *The Glorious Oak*. I baulked at first, not having Gloinn's self-confidence, but Larry was happy for me to write occasional poems in Irish. One of the first I wrote, *Claiomh Na Brigidin* (*The Sword of St Brigid*), caused a slight difference of opinion between Larry and myself. He claimed that St Brigid, since she was a woman, wouldn't have owned a sword. At best, in order to protect herself, or for domestic or recreational purposes, such as carving her name into a tree, she would have carried a small knife. Furthermore, as an independent single woman living alone (I don't quite know where he got this information – St Brigid is generally regarded as being semi-mythical), he thought it unlikely that she would have borrowed a sword from a friend or neighbour. I disagreed, and stressed that my poem was, in any case, largely metaphorical. Larry, after an intervention from Gloinn, eventually relented and the poem was published.

Larry's tireless work for the poor was legendary. Apart from his own selfless efforts in the inner city, he spent much of his adult life (until ill health forced him to slow down about twenty years ago) organizing charitable events to raise money for the less well off. His celebrity 'fun runs' during the 1970s and early 1980s were memorable occasions. And who else but Larry could have persuaded Sean Connery and the Reverend Ian Paisley to take part in the same event?!

Larry himself suffered some hard times during the last decade, and in 1992 was evicted from his corporation house for non-payment of rent. It seems extraordinary that none of his many friends (and I am afraid I must include myself here) were willing to pay the arrears of ten pounds which would have saved him having to struggle along as a down-and-out. Gloinn, who had been away from the country for a while, met him at this time, and made an unfortunate faux pas. He came across Larry in the street, and happened to mention that things must have been going well for him, as he'd heard he'd been seen in a Mitsubishi car. In fact, Larry had been living in a cardboard box from an old Mitsubishi washing machine.

As I write, Larry, at the age of well over a hundred, is still forced to fend for himself on the streets. Last year, he was set upon by a group of English youths attending a stag party in the Temple Bar area who mocked his accent, called him 'Paddy', branded the words 'Combat 18' on his arm with a hot iron, poured petrol over him and then set him on fire. He was left with no option but to throw himself into the freezing canal to save his own life. (This incident

provided the title for Gloinn's recently published book on Republicanism, *The Extinguished Flame*.) Dublin Corporation, his old employer, still refuses to rehouse him until the outstanding ten pounds is paid, and no one, including his friends (of whom I am proud to be one) and the many hundreds of people he has helped over the years, seems willing to step forward and come up with the amount.

On the day Hitler came to power in Germany, 30 January 1933, I married Noreen in the Church of the Sacred Heart, Naas. My wife (I got a huge laugh from all our guests at the subsequent reception when I very purposely referred to her using that term!) looked gorgeous in her wedding dress, and I knew I had made the 'right choice' when she arrived at my side in the church. The celebrant was Noreen's uncle, Father Pat Quigley, a lovely fellow, who tragically died in the Congo some years ago while piloting a light aircraft, something he was ill-qualified to attempt. (The unfortunate result, I later found out, of an over-confident bet made while he was very drunk. Sadly, it also transpired that he was 'sozzled' while at the controls; at least twenty times over the legal limit for flying planes.) My best man, of course, was Gloinn, who accompanied us on our honeymoon to Kildare town and stayed with us in the Fox's Arms Hotel for the duration, often popping into the marital bed with myself and Noreen when the winter nights got particularly cold. Once, while I was in the toilet at the end of the corridor outside the bedroom, he tried to have sex with Noreen. I was a bit annoyed with him at first, but when he told me that it was Noreen who had led him on, I accepted his explanation immediately. Over the years, I have often wondered if Gloinn was being slightly disingenuous about this, as Noreen has the sexual urges of a corpse. However, I'm sure my best man was probably telling the truth, and in fact it is now something we often give each other a gentle ribbing about!

Around this time, Gloinn had started 'doing a line' with Maire, and was as keen for me to consent in his choice as I was eager for him to give the 'stamp of approval' to Noreen. His fiancée came to visit us in Kildare, and the first thing I remember about her was her glasses, which she had made herself out of sticks and the bottoms of jam-jars. She apologized profusely about this, but her usual spectacles had been crushed under a lorry, and her sight was so bad she had felt it necessary to make an improvised pair herself. It was also evident on our first meeting that her hair was growing completely wild, and it looked as though she had never had a haircut of any sort, or indeed had even washed her hair, in her entire life. (Gloinn confirmed this to me shortly after their marriage.) I think it's fair to say that even Maire herself would agree that she also is a 'stocky' woman, and even in her mid-twenties she would have weighed upwards of fifteen stone. However, as I have mentioned earlier, Gloinn himself is no 'oil painting', and their marriage is based on common intellectual pursuits (such as regular games of cards) and a mutual religious devotion, rather than a Richard Burton/Liz Taylor type attraction. 'Ah, sure she's someone to talk to,'

Gloinn has often remarked defensively when people – often complete strangers – have come up to him to ask how he got lumbered with such a woman. This is a hollow excuse, I always feel, as one could say the same thing about a dog or a cat. (Many people are also surprised that she is a woman, as she looks more like a man, or, in an unflattering light, some type of ape.) One entrepreneur once approached Gloinn, while himself and Maire were on a pilgrimage to Rome, and asked him if he would be interested in selling her to a circus that he had a connection with. Gloinn has admitted to me that he did not immediately dismiss the suggestion out of hand, but Maire was having none of it, and made a big scene in St Peter's Square. Gloinn did say to me years later that he thought Maire might have been happier living in a cage and having the World's Hairiest Man and the Leopard Woman for companions. I agreed with him that they sounded more like her intellectual peer group.

A funny incident happened once when 'The Odd Couple' – as my brother Brian used to call them – hired a caravan to travel around Kerry. Maire travelled in the caravan (she was too big to fit in their Ford Escort), and when they went over a pothole was thrown into the air. When she landed, the axle could not withstand the full weight of her – she could have been up to twenty-two or -three stone at this stage – and snapped in two. I know Gloinn must have lost his temper over this incident, because afterwards she would often bring it up in conversation when she required a favour off him.

Let us pause now for a short time to study further the man who is Gloinn McTire. To pass him in the street, you would say he was unremarkable. Of slightly less than average height (Gloinn always used to say, 'What's average?!'), you would not fail to notice that he is immaculately turned out. At home, while relaxing in his armchair reading a newspaper or watching a programme on the Irish language television channel, T4G, he may wear a casual light blue or beige coloured sweater or cardigan – admittedly always with a shirt and tie – but as he makes his way between his various committees, societies and organizations, you will never see him wearing anything other than a formal suit of brown or statesman-like black. Like many an elderly man, strange white hairs have started to grow on the tip of his reddish nose, and you will notice that his fingers (and, strangely, thumbs) are yellow from the stains of nicotine. The once jet-black hair which jutted up sharply from his head has now mostly gone. What little he has left has turned a solemn grey. Chatting to him on the street when even a light gale is blowing, you will see him push back the remaining strands across his head at regular intervals, now as much out of habit as an attempt to enforce some discipline over his unruly mop.

To get to know Gloinn may take some time. The exterior appearance hides a spirit of indomitable will and dogged determination. Scourge of the liberal agenda, enemy of the contraceptive society, he speaks his mind with courage and conviction, even if many do not wish to listen to his message. Not for nothing has he recently become the first man to be called a c**t live on national television. He has a passion for his country and his religion that is lamentably rare in these dark days.

He tries to live a frugal life, and this has sometimes led to unfortunate accusations of meanness from people who do not know him as intimately as his closest friends. However, even he himself would admit that he is 'careful' with money, and a telltale sign of his thriftiness is the fact that when himself and Maire go on holidays, he removes the batteries in their household clocks for the duration of their absence.

I have seen every side of Gloinn over the years. His proudest moment was when he was elected for Fianna Fail in the by-election for Laois/Offaly in 1954. Alas, his time in Dail Eireann was not to last long, but I agree with him (and the newspaper pundits) that he made his mark. But the ending of a political career only gave him more time: to organize; to galvanize; to defend. Perhaps the low point of his life was the incident I have already described; drinking lamp oil in that lovely cathedral in Lausanne. But there have been many highs. When we greeted the Holy Father in Maynooth in 1979, it was an unforgettable moment we shared together. He believes he has a mission in life: it has been my privilege to accompany him on the path.

In 1935, myself, Gloinn and Larry Hoey (as honourable chairman) founded the League of the Mother of God against Sin. It was the first of many organizations, magazines and pressure groups I was involved in with Gloinn over the years. Both of us had been very much of the same mind for some time: we did not wish to see anti-

Irish and anti-Catholic forces emerge without any agencies to combat their propaganda. It is important to remember that Communism was a very real threat at the time – nowhere more so than in Ireland – and its messages of anti-clericalism and contempt for Christianity were anathema to the average citizen. Gloinn and myself were among the first people, after the Bishops, to spot the dangers posed by such anti-Gaelic influences as jazz music and modern dancing. In fact, Gloinn may have been slightly ahead of the Bishops in spotting the menace of jazz. I remember him alerting Cardinal MacRory, in a spirited letter to Armagh, about a 'Dixieland' record which had been played on Radio Eireann. This, admittedly, turned out to have been a genuine error on the broadcaster's behalf. The man, a good Catholic, had been having mental troubles at the time and was not in control of his actions. Gloinn, myself and (of course) the Bishops, knew that jazz and modern dancing would lead to an open attitude towards sex, thus negating the Church's role in society. The League, an organization which soon attracted many concerned citizens, was to play a pivotal role in stemming the tide against liberalism over the coming years. This has not made either me or Gloinn popular in the anti-Catholic media. In fact, the popular perception of Gloinn as – and I quote directly from a recent letter in *The Irish Times* – 'a f***ing crackpot' stems from this hostility.

As Michael Judge explained to me all those years ago, sex is indeed a bit of a 'hornets' nest'. By mutual consent (not to say relief!), myself and Noreen had agreed not to consummate our marriage until we had received counsel and instruction from my parish priest, Father Gerry Dawson. Father Dawson was a greatly experienced cleric (he would have been well into his seventies at the time), and we knew he would keep us on the 'straight and narrow'. I recall him listening with great interest to my views on the subject as he munched expensive Belgian chocolates and sipped sherry from a beautiful Waterford Crystal glass which he had got from nuns in Cabra on the occasion of the fiftieth anniversary of his ordination. I told him that when I was young I had seen two dogs copulating in a field, and whenever I contemplated myself having intercourse, this was an image that automatically came into my head. He nodded and smiled understandingly, as if this was something he identified with.

After a thorough interrogation from Father D., who took a particular interest in Noreen's innermost sexual thoughts, constantly urging her on to reveal more – she went bright red throughout! – we looked forward to hearing his words of wisdom. Of course, his advice was just great. He told us (meaning me) not to make a move (on Noreen) until 'the time was right', and that we would only find that out through 'the goodness of God'. It would have been hard to imagine a more clear or straightforward piece of advice from anyone, and we remained grateful to Father Dawson for the rest of our married lives. Myself and my new bride felt like a weight had been lifted off our shoulders as we left his beautiful church in the North Strand. From that day on we were able to skip gaily along the path of married life free of the burden of physical desire. Of course, I knew that the time would never be 'right' for a move on Noreen, and I was thankful that one of the greatest gifts I could give to my new wife would be to free her from the threat of sexual conquest; the 'lurking dark beast' that has wrecked so many other marriages.

Without the distractions of sex to trouble us, or indeed any type of manifestation or display of physical affection – Gloinn once said to me that the nearest Noreen and I got to having sex was when she waved at me as I left the house to go to work! – I was able to concentrate on my duties in the department. Meanwhile, Noreen, who had quite properly given up her nursing career, busied herself making a comfortable home for the two of us in a rented house in Sandymount. We had no furniture, except for an old cardboard shoebox, and I remember a lot of standing around for the first year. Although we were desperate to have children, we were equally desperate not to have sex, so we decided to adopt. We were told that there was a long waiting list, but early in 1937, a man dropped over our first child, Lorcan, to us in a van. Lorcan (bizarrely) looked just like Noreen, and we loved him from the first moment we saw his little face. I have always enjoyed the innocence of children, and could write an entire book about the funny things that Lorcan, and later our daughter Sorcha, would say to us. I remember on one occasion having to take them to a cartoon film in about 1940 and watching the newsreel beforehand. I think it must have been around the time that Hitler invaded Holland and Belgium, because there on screen, in typical confident pose, was the German main man, looking out at his adoring audience in Berlin or somewhere. The cinema was very quiet at the time, and lo and behold didn't little Lorcan suddenly yell out the word 'tits'. I really didn't know quite where to look as the other bemused cinema-goers glanced around to see where the cry had come from. I also had to explain to the little fellow later that as we were a staunchly Republican family, our sympathies lay firmly with 'Mein Fuhrer' (Hitler).

While I admired much about the German leader, and obviously supported him in the war against British imperialism, I did have reservations about some of his social and foreign policies. Gloinn, however, would never hear a word against 'the little Austrian'. In fact, during this period, as part of his duties in the Department of Education, where he had been translating a handbook about pole-vaulting into Irish, Gloinn accompanied the national team to the Berlin Olympic Games. (These were the Games where Hitler, rather unwisely, decided to take on the black athlete Jesse Owens in the final of the one hundred metres in an ill-judged attempt to demonstrate the superiority of the Aryan race. He looked more than a little foolish when he finished a very poor second to the famous American runner.) Gloinn came back impressed with the country and with a great story to tell; he had actually met Hitler when the Great Dictator dropped in unexpectedly to the team's HQ on a courtesy call. Knowing Gloinn as I do, I suspect the Master

Orator and Man Behind the Third Reich hardly got a word in! Apparently, Gloinn bombarded Hitler with a long diatribe about what he would do if he were in charge of Irish language policy in the Fianna Fail government. Hitler, unsurprisingly, had little interest in this, but promised that if he ever invaded Ireland, he'd look Gloinn up, and the two men parted on friendly terms. Gloinn wrote to him for months afterwards, and later, during the war, sent him 'good luck' telegrams during the battles of Stalingrad and Kursk.

Gloinn in his book on Hitler (*The Man Behind the Third Reich*) bemoans the fact that the German leader didn't marry earlier. His bachelor status, according to Gloinn, 'didn't suit him', and a happier home life might have made all the difference between winning and losing against the Allies. The few hours of married life that he did spend with Eva Braun (I wonder if he, like I did at my wedding, got a laugh at their sad little reception in the Fuhrerbunker by referring to her as 'my wife') must have been unbearably poignant. I can't imagine a worse start to a marriage than, instead of flying off on a nice honeymoon to Spain or Portugal, having to kill yourself after first instructing your adjutant to pour petrol over your newly wed/dead body and burn it so that it will become unrecogizable. After the Fuhrer's death, myself and Gloinn, following de Valera's brave and noble lead, called into the German embassy in Dublin to pay our respects. There was, quite understandably, a very sombre mood present that day. I remember a very grumpy Nazi-type on reception, and thinking that he would have been more suited to a job rounding up and hanging partisans on the Eastern Front. (This is a thought that has often occurred to me over the years when I have come into contact with some of our own rather self-import-ant and unhelpful Irish civil servants!) We said a few prayers for Hitler and left shortly afterwards.

Ireland, like many countries in Europe, had its fair share of admirers of strong leadership as personified by Hitler and Mussolini. This period saw the rise of the Blueshirts, under the leadership of General Eoin O'Duffy, a War of Independence veteran who had taken the pro-Treaty side in the civil war. (Recent revelations – for once not concerning a bishop – describe an unlikely love affair between O'Duffy and the notorious homosexual founder of the Gate Theatre, Michael MacLiammoir; a fact not surprisingly played down in O'Duffy's election literature of the time.) As both myself and Gloinn were 'Dev men', there was no question that we would join the Blueshirts, though there was much to admire about their anti-Communism and desire to reunite the country using extreme violence against the Northern Prods. The Blue-shirt meetings were often disrupted by IRA men and de Valera supporters, and I have dug up a cutting from *The Irish Independent* which gives an accurate flavour of the times. It describes incidents at a meeting in Dunleer, Co. Louth, in 1934.

General O'Duffy took the platform under a hail of beetroot, which came from a section of the crowd consisting of Mr de Valera's supporters. He began by stating that he would not be denied free speech by cowards and gunmen. (Voice from crowd: 'Who is the gunman now!?') This pronounce-ment by General O'Duffy was greeted with loud cheering by his supporters. The General continued by referring to Mr de Valera as 'a Frenchman [sic], a tamperer with constitu-tionalism, a limbo-brained ferret licker, and a jazz singer.' At this point a hen was thrown on to the platform to sounds of clucking and jeers from the crowd. The hen proceeded to chase General O'Duffy around the platform for several minutes. (Voice from crowd: 'It's the hen that has you on the run now, O'Duffy!') At this point shots were fired and skirmishes erupted at the side of the plat-form. (Voice from crowd: 'Who put the millstone around Robert Emmet's neck!?')

General O'Duffy was unable to continue his speech and left shortly afterwards for a shopping expedition to Ardee.

Gloinn and myself witnessed similar scenes when we were part of a pro-Fianna Fáil crowd disrupting a Blue-shirt rally at Greystones, Co. Wicklow, early the follow-ing year. I remember the unpleasant – but curiously entertaining – spectacle of a pet tortoise belonging to General O'Duffy being stamped on by a group of IRA men until it was completely flat. It was then thrown, frisbee-like, over a nearby wall. The General must have been furious, as I found out later that he had been very fond of the tortoise, and during the War of Indepen-dence they had been in several scrapes together. With typical humour, he had even given it the nickname 'Dev'.

CHAPTER 4

Home Amongst the Clouds

Early in 1938, I applied for and was granted a job on the National Censorship Board, which had been founded some years before after a recommendation by the Committee on Evil Literature, a body formed to combat the influx of modern novels and stupid ideas into the country. There were a number of vacancies on the board, and Gloinn also put his name forward. Happily, his application was also successful, and in February that year we found ourselves working together for the first time. This was a welcome opportunity for both of us to put some of our ideas about the moral and cultural climate of the country into action. A year or two earlier, Gloinn had found a copy of James Joyce's *Ulysses* in a pub toilet and couldn't believe some of the things in it. He showed it to me, and neither of us could understand how the human brain could come up with such filth. What made the matter even more peculiar was the fact that Joyce was a Catholic. Irish filth was usually produced by Protestants such as Samuel Beckett or Oscar Wilde. Ould Jimmy Joyce certainly deserves his position as one of Ireland's premier pornographers, and over the course of the last one hundred years only Ranger MacWoods – of whom we will hear more later – has rivalled him in the filth stakes. Eventually, after reading as much as we could stand of his revolting novel – about three pages – we flushed the dirty book down the toilet from whence it came. Nowadays, the Irish ten punt note features a picture of James Joyce. It seems that it is now the country that has gone down the jacks.*

Our job on the board was simple: to ban as many books as possible. Our immediate superior, Sean Lennon, encouraged us in our work, often telling us that if the title or cover illustration of a book was suspicious, we could ban it without reading it. I have to admit that we used to have tremendous fun. Even if we didn't ban a book outright, we could still render it meaningless by dipping our pens constantly into the numerous bottles of red ink and deleting entire chapters at a time. Socialists such as Sean O'Faolain must have been driven mad by our relentless, indiscriminate censorship! Certainly, for example, I never read any of his books, and usually banned them outright without even looking at the title. Many of the dirtiest books weren't actually novels, but self-styled 'academic' works. For example, anything that masqueraded as a treatise on 'population control' (on the face of it, a very non-titillating subject) was almost certainly a propagandist work in favour of contraception (a very big 'turn on' indeed).

We had to be very wary of many authors who would try to use the publication of a supposedly educational book as 'the thin end of the wedge' for more 'hardcore'

* See *Ireland in Crisis* by Eoin O'Ceallaigh (Dunbeg Press, Cork, 1996).

works. After he had sneaked his 'academic book' through the door, thus gaining some sort of dubious respectability, the unscrupulous scribe would invariably attempt to follow it with a work of disgusting erotic fiction, featuring passages describing lovemaking and abortion practices. This was a tactic attempted by almost all Irish 'intellectual' authors during our time on the board. I remember one fellow who went to the trouble of getting a science degree in Trinity College just so he could write a scholarly work on biology. Needless to say, when his second book arrived on our desk, we quickly discovered that it was more or less a complete *paean* to the pleasures of the blow job. We became very wise to this ploy over the years.

Working on the board also allowed Gloinn and myself to promote some of our own works. My first book of poetry, *Ruathai Amach* (*Bicycles Outside*), was published in early 1939, while Gloinn's *The Lumpen Communist* first saw the light of day later the same year. This was quickly followed by two works of non-fiction by Gloinn, *Christ Almighty* and *Counterblast*. The latter book sold particularly well, part of the reason being that even though it was a passionate argument against the onspread of liberalism, many people thought it was an espionage novel.

Working during the war in the early forties also allowed us an even greater excuse to ban things, as we could justify almost anything for 'reasons of national security'.

The Taoiseach, Eamon de Valera, encouraged us

greatly in our work. His recent constitution made it plain that Ireland would be no place for the non-Catholic, and he saw us as important cogs in the machine of anti-pluralism. I was to meet often with him over the years, and was impressed by the Long Fellow, not least because I identified with him in so many ways. He was, of course, an out and out Republican, until pragmatism forced him to take the constitutional path. However, he saw no room for compromise when it came to his religion. I once asked him if he was forced to make a choice between God and country, which one would he choose. He didn't pause for a second before replying that since God and Ireland were on the same side, he would never be put in such a position. There could be no doubt about that, he said. It would not be like arguing over a kick-in at a football match. It was a clever response. I had to agree that he was right.

I remember having to hide a dirty book on masturbation rituals amongst the Indo-Chinese which I was reading when Dev popped into the board one afternoon. I was sure that he would not be familiar either with the word or its practice, and I didn't want to get into the position of having to describe the awfulness of the subject to him in all its lurid detail. (De Valera, with his famously meticulous – ironically, almost Protestant-like – mind, would have required a comprehensive report.) Gloinn, on a later occasion, was not so lucky. The first book describing oral pleasure between men had somehow arrived in our office, and Mr McT. was giving it the once over. As I remember, like most dirty books, it had a rather innocent title: something like *What John Did to Tom*. Dev drifted in unexpectedly after lunch, caught Gloinn reading it, asked him what it was about, and mentioned that he was looking for a book to give to his wife Sinead as a present for Christmas. Would the thing Gloinn was reading be suitable? If you can remember Sinead de Valera – a tiny, feeble, white-haired woman who contented herself writing unfrightening Irish ghost stories – then you can only imagine the effect that a book describing 'oral' between men might have on her. Gloinn, highly flustered and completely stuck for words, accidentally dropped the book on the floor, and unfortunately Dev picked it up. I still remember the tension in the office as he slowly read some pages, his long figure hunched over Gloinn's desk. Neither Gloinn nor I dared speak. For what seemed like an eternity, the old 1916 commandant studied the text. I do not know if Dev played cards (I suspect he did not – it would be far too frivolous an occupation for his brilliant mind), but the term 'poker face' would have been a fair description of his expression as he concentrated on the work before him. The descriptive passages he was immersed in would have felled a lesser man, but not a flicker crossed the Chief's face. My only hope, and in the climate of the time it was not an unrealistic one, was that Dev would not know what a 'penis' was. However, I realized the game was up when I caught sight of two words on the cover that said simply 'illustrated edition'. As if detailed descriptions weren't distressing enough, actual illustrations would have surely floored Bean de Valera should the book have ended up in her Christmas stocking. However, this was not a likely scenario once Dev snapped the book shut. 'Perhaps not,' he said. 'Maybe you could find me a book on Clare folklore?'

During the war, Larry, Gloinn, Maire, Noreen and myself made a marvellous first pilgrimage to Lough Mullet in Co. Mayo. (We would make the trip many more times over the coming years.) The monastery there was very popular with Irish people at the time, and was a place of fasting, prayer and penitention. There really was, as it said in its beautifully produced promotional brochure, 'everything for the Catholic', including barefoot walking (through mud), praying, going to mass and chatting with priests. Our own little gang from Dublin was led by Father Gerry Dawson, who, as I mentioned earlier, did much to encourage Noreen and I not to have sex. Larry, typically, wanted to go for a month, but that was too like going in at the 'deep end', so we settled for a fortnight.

The Monastery was on a tiny island in the middle of the Lough. The only boat available to pilgrims had been vandalized (by Protestants?) on the day we arrived, so access to the site would be difficult. Some people elected to swim over, but our group waited for low tide and waded out through the water. This turned out to be a five or six mile hike, and I can still recall our little heads bobbing up and down over the gentle waves of that beautiful Lough. We had, at Larry's suggestion, also elected to walk out fully clothed, and offer up the discomfort of drenched garments to the Holy Souls in

Purgatory when we reached the island. I don't know, dear reader, if you have ever worn wet clothes for a fortnight – the damp weather had the effect of constantly 'topping up' our discomfort – but I reckon a few Holy Souls may have had their remand period considerably shortened by our efforts.

Once on the island, Larry couldn't wait to walk barefoot up Mount Cloghey, an impressive man-made hill of sticks, nettles, shit, razor blades and broken glass. The rest of us opted for a straightforward, no-frills mass, but Larry, impatient as ever when it came to punishing himself for spiritual gain, immediately set off to 'do Cloghey'. We didn't see him again till later that night, when he proudly boasted that he had climbed the hill four times in three hours, something that had never been achieved before. His feet, not surprisingly, were completely shredded: a mess of blood, flapping skin, burst veins and mangled toes that seemed to merge into one another. (Gloinn thought he would have been able to use them as flippers!) Larry would make the same ascent every day of our visit, and always seemed invigorated by his achievement. The constant mass-going and confession-making also caused an extraordinary state of euphoria in Larry. As he said himself, 'I'm as high as a kite!'

Gloinn and I, despite our strong religious devotion, were in the ha'penny place compared to our old friend. The League had been a great success, and at the time we went to Lough Mullet, membership numbered several hundred. Larry always led a full rosary before our meetings, held in a church hall in Parnell Street. He was meticulous about every word, and if he felt a decade hadn't gone particularly well, he would say the whole thing again. This often led to fifty decades or more being said, with the result that often the real business of the meeting had to be postponed.

People often remarked on Larry's trousers. He spent so much time on his knees praying, that he had special reinforced knee pads made by a nun from the convent in Clanbrassil Street. This was fine, until one day he got the idea that it would be a great plan to remove the knee pads and replace them with Brillo pads. The suffering inflicted by wiry bits of twisted metal tearing into the knee really appealed to him, and he noticed that by grinding his knees into the pads, he could 'up' the agony factor even further. For a time gutters were installed in the pews in St Anthony's Church in Fairview to take away the blood pouring from Larry's knees. Meanwhile, of course, prayers flowed out the other end of him in equal measure.

I mentioned earlier myself and Noreen's own lack of furniture when we moved into our house in Sandy-mount. But while our situation was rectified after a while, Larry, in the many years I have known him, has always refused to own any household items at all. 'The tiniest discomfort is a gift to God' was his constant mantra. I remember the time he had a central-heating system installed in his tiny flat in Ringsend. This surprised me greatly, because I knew he welcomed the freezing cold when it came every winter, and enjoyed sitting in his underwear in the corner of his room during the long, dark evenings reading the latest overseas bulletin from the medical missionaries in Africa. However, he explained to me that he would only turn on the heating during very hot days in the summer, so that he could suffer the torment of searing heat as the temperatures soared to the very levels of hell itself.

He also inflicted agonies on himself in other ways. When he was starving with the hunger, after a week or more's fasting, he would prepare himself a lovely tea of sausages, eggs, rashers and toast. He'd sniff at it for a time, enjoying the smells and aromas wafting up from the plate, and then, without any outward display of emotion, throw the whole lot into the bin. Perhaps the most spectacular act he ever did was to nail himself to the kitchen door. This self-crucifixion was extraordinary in its barbarity. He succeeded in first nailing his feet to the bottom of the door before proceeding to impale his left hand, a task that took him several hours of increasingly wayward hammering. One can only imagine the excruciating pain. This, of course, left him in the difficult position of nailing his right hand to the door, but since this was his 'hammer hand', it proved an impossible task. He hung there for a week, until discovered by an anxious neighbour. He told me afterwards that he'd loved every minute of it. He was also thrilled that as a result of deliberately using rusty nails he'd contracted a severe bout of tetanus.

Though I absolutely admire his achievements, I have never quite had Larry's extraordinary application to self-torture. I like to think that I serve God in a different, and certainly less bloody, way. My work at the Censorship Board I definitely saw as a way of keeping the devil at bay. Over the coming years the battle would intensify.

I have not yet described in great detail my wife Noreen, or indeed Gloinn's 'better half', Maire. Since their lives are inextricably linked, and as it is my belief that women generally share the same characteristics and personalities, for the purposes of this profile I shall 'lump them together'.

Until Noreen died in the summer of 1981, both ladies were the best of pals. They were each deeply devoted to their respective husbands, and knew that the first duty of the wife is to provide a happy home for her spouse. As we are both 'workaholics' (and Gloinn an occasional 'alcoholic'!), and expect the same amount of zeal in others, this role was never easy for either of them, especially Maire, who is prone to stupefying laziness.

Neither woman could have been called attractive. I have said to Gloinn, in a bid to cheer him up in recent years when he has remarked wearily on the mind-numbing plainness of Maire's looks, that she looked so bad in the first place that the ageing process has made no practical difference. I know she will not mind me saying that on several occasions she has caused car crashes on account of her unaccountably odd facial characteristics. Gloinn believes that she can turn milk sour (or possibly into yoghurt) by looking at it. Noreen, thankfully, was never so utterly awful looking, but was certainly no matinee idol. I think it's fair to say as well that her personality was unspectacular. And yet, there was something about her that made her a decent woman. I think she knew from early on that the main thing was not to have any expectations from life. She knew that she was stuck with her load, and she just had to 'get on with it'. This was a great 'plus'. During our marriage, she was to suffer from one illness after another, and I often asked God what I had done to deserve all the pain and inconvenience. However, I was lucky that, unlike Maire, she had many of the talents that help a woman to become a good wife. She was very well organized: for example, the house was never short of biscuits should a visitor drop in unexpectedly, and we rarely ran out of toilet paper. (On the one occasion this did happen, Val Doonican – of all people – happened to be visiting. It was very embarrassing for everybody when he called down the stairs, alerting us to the problem.) Another one of Noreen's priorities in life was to keep a supply of sherry in the living-room cabinet. Although neither one of us took a drink, a priest or bishop was always likely to drop by. Once, a Vincentian father happened to come home with me after a conference. He had such an almighty thirst for the Cockburn's that Noreen had to make a hasty visit to the nearest bar to top up the supply. I believe it was the only time in her life that she was inside a public house.

She was also handy with a needle, could cook a nice tea, and used to love knitting. I remember, in the days before television, coming home in the evenings and listening to the wireless while Noreen busied herself with her long, grey knitting needles which her mother had won in a talent competition. During the Cuban missile crisis in 1962, I have a distinct memory of being literally glued to Radio Eireann, listening to all the latest news coming in from Washington. Would the Russians force Kennedy's hand? Would the planet be consumed by nuclear war? Noreen, typically, was oblivious to it all. She had no thought in her mind other than how she was going to get some cardigan or jumper done by the weekend. On another occasion, the details of which I forget, I had to call her from America at three o'clock in the morning (Irish time) and ask her to hurriedly darn a pair of my socks. She did so immediately and uncomplainingly.

Simple thoughts of children, husband and home filled her mind. Prayer and religion, of course, was also very important in her life, but Noreen had the great gift of taking Catholicism seriously without philosophizing about it, something that women, I believe, have a particular talent for. It is, of course, the true meaning of faith.

Nowadays, I think the 'gentler sex' have rather too much on their minds. I have often thought that their natural reaction is to be frightened if a complex thought accidentally flutters into their little heads. A philosophical concept can have the same effect on them as seeing a mouse or a bat. Their instinct is to immediately jump up on a chair or

to run from the house. And yet, increasingly, we see women being encouraged to think deeply about complicated or intricate subjects, when it is plainly obvious that exposure to such matters can only leave them confused or disorientated. Often on television discussion programmes nowadays, I hear the prefix 'professor' before a lady is introduced. (Indeed the most recent Irish lady president is a 'professor' of some description.) Whenever I hear this term, I picture a crusty, bespectacled old timer in a white coat peering down a microscope in a laboratory at a cross-section of a mouse's brain. It is more than a shock to see the professor revealed on screen as a girl in her twenties. When asked for their opinions, these colleens tend to become at best, confused, at worst, totally bewildered. It may make for fine spectator sport, but in the long term I think it is a sign that society has taken yet another wrong turn. Despite all the feminist 'hype', it is sobering to reflect on the fact that during the last one hundred years, in the fields of science, technology, the arts and politics, the contribution of women has been absolutely nil. Recently, I met a former female member of the Dail who had won her seat in one of the many elections held during the 1980s. She secretly confided to me that on reflection, she believed that representing the public was 'no job for a woman'. Furthermore, she told me that although she could never admit it in public, she had come to the conclusion that in many ways it would have been better if women had never been granted the right to vote at all.

I remember a couple of years ago seeing the President of Pakistan on television; an attractive girl going under the unlikely name of 'Benazir Bhutto'. She was at some conference or other; giving out about this and that, saying she was going to do all these great things for Pakistan. Gloinn was watching with me, and after she had listed all her great plans for giant dams, military expansion and nuclear bombs, he turned to me and said, 'That's all very well, but who's going to make the dinner in their house?' I had to laugh. It was amusing indeed to picture in my mind's eye poor 'Mr Bhutto' overturning saucepans and searching frantically through cupboards as he tried to knock himself together a half-decent chicken curry!

Home life changed again with the arrival of our little daughter, Sorcha, some time in the late thirties. She too, like Lorcan, was delivered in a van from the orphanage with the minimum of fuss. I think we only ever had to fill out two forms to get Sorcha. I recall the day of her christening being a grand day out, and memorable for another incident: Gloinn told me he'd decided to join the IRA. Father Gerry Dawson, wildly drunk, did 'the honours' at the christening, and afterwards everyone headed back to our house for some tea and ham sandwiches. It was later that evening when Gloinn told me that he wanted to take a more active part in the national struggle, and did I know anyone with a gun? I said that surely the IRA would supply guns to their volunteers, but Gloinn said no. He'd met 'a man' in Skerries who said that if he wanted to join the IRA, he'd have to bring his own gun. Gloinn looked around for a while to see if he could lay his hands on even a small revolver, but could never find one. His nephew had a toy pistol that fired caps, but it was unfortunately incapable of fulfilling the main purpose of a real firearm: killing people. (Gloinn did have a grand time, though, posing with it in front of the mirror and pretending to be Michael Collins.) He finally said to the 'man' that he would have no problem getting his hands on sharp sticks, or even some pokers, but in the end he was told more or less to feck off. He then volunteered to start fires or give people lifts in his car, but I don't think anything came of it. In the end, he joined Fianna Fail instead.

Around the same time, we both became active members of the Gaelic Athletic Association. Gaelic football, in particular, to those who are not fans, may seem like a primitive, violent, mindless exercise in unspeakable brutality. However, to the initiated enthusiast, it's all this and more. Gloinn and myself enjoyed our frequent visits to Croke Park where we would cheer on the Dublin teams in both hurling and football with great gusto. During one of these matches, I met The Rooster for the first time since I had left school. He appeared noticeably older and walked with a limp. I asked if something had happened to his leg. Yes, he said, it had had to be amputated some months previously when he'd badly mangled it after he'd thrown himself off the roof of St Fintan's. It was only afterwards that I realized that this must have been a suicide attempt. Why else would you throw yourself off a roof? This was, after all, in the days before bungee jumping became popular with Christian

Brothers.* Was it a cry for help, perhaps, or a genuine attempt to extinguish a bright life that for whatever reason had dimmed? The fact that the roof at St Fintan's was at least ninety feet high led me to the latter conclusion. (Luckily, a passing 'roly-poly' Friar Tuck-type Brother had cushioned The Rooster's fall.) I lost track of my old tutor after that meeting, but later heard he died sometime in the 1960s. His latter years were apparently sad ones, and by the time of his death he had become a melancholy and lonely figure around the school.

A couple of years earlier, he had foolishly put his life savings on a horse to win at Punchestown races after meeting a man in a pub where he had popped in to buy matches. (Like me, he was a lifelong teetotaller.) Up until then he had never made a bet in his life, but the man said sure wouldn't it be a great thrill for an elderly Brother to ring up a bookie, put his entire life savings on the horse, called Booster's Shoe-In, and then watch the race on the television which was bolted high up on a wall in the corner of the pub over the advertisement for Sweet Afton cigarettes. 'And sure why not have a packet of crisps and a 7-Up as well? . . . And, since you're ordering, I'll have a pint of Guinness.' The Rooster, flattered by the attention and unused to the high life, must have felt like Frank Sinatra in Las Vegas. 'Why not indeed?' he said. 'I've got nothing to lose!' (In fact, he had his entire life savings to lose.) Things initially were

* See *Down, Up, and a Decade of the Rosary: The Christian Brothers and Bungee Jumping in Ireland* by Desmond McKeeb (Trinity Press, Tralee, 1997).

going well, and the nag was winning all the way until it keeled over and died seconds away from the winning post. To add insult to injury, the man who had urged him to make the bet then laughed in his face. Booster's Shoe-In had unfortunately become Rooster's Ruin! Needless to say, this had been an experience which shook the old Brother greatly to the extent that he was ultimately forced to take his own life. I remember Gloinn remarking to me that the mythical (or, in this case, non-mythical) 'man in a pub' had claimed another victim.

CHAPTER 5

The Whittling Curtain

Have you ever been to Co. Wexford? I suppose it is possible, dear reader, that you may even live there. It is a remarkable part of the country for many reasons. For me, it has always been a place of significance because of its place in Irish nationalist history. The 1798 rebellion was largely fought in the locality, and I have often visited the battlefields at Oulart and Vinegar Hill. I happened to be driving through Enniscorthy sometime in the summer of 1946, on one such visit, when I accidentally took a wrong turning and ended up on a back road to Carlow. Some miles out of the town, I spotted a ruined cottage on a hill. A strange sensation – an indescribable enchantment which I can still recollect over fifty years later – gripped me, and I felt compelled to leave the car to have a closer look. I walked up the hill until I noticed, at the gate leading up to the ruin, a rather old For Sale sign. When I reached the front door, I opened it, and the handle came off in my hand, while the decaying door itself fell away from its hinges. Inside, long grass grew where there was once a floor, but the fireplace was still intact. Gaps in the roof let in the only light, as all the windows were heavily boarded up. I realized, though, that this cottage had a perceptible, yet indeterminate charm. I found myself imagining the people that had lived within its whitewashed walls. Very probably the last occupants had been forced by necessity to emigrate across the sea like so many billions of others before them. Now all that was left of their home was this dank, crumbling, yet strangely atmospheric, ruin.

For some time, I had been thinking of moving away from Dublin and living in a more rural environment. Like Pearse, I believed that the true spirit of the Irish nation was to be found amongst the mountains, fields, valleys and occasional hills of the countryside. I suddenly fell in love with the idea of living in this simple labourer's cottage. In my head, I started composing a poem about the place, *Muhai Beag An Teach* (*The Little Ruined Cottage*).

> *Little ruined cottage,*
> *With your white walls,*
> *Don't cry for me, Argentina,*
> *My home is by the old bog road.*

It would take great physical effort and dedication to make the little hovel inhabitable, but I am a determined individual who has never been afraid of hard work. I resolved that the next weekend I would drive Noreen down, and show her my lovely little cottage. When I arrived back in Dublin she readily agreed that it would be worth seeing – luckily, she also had ambitions to live away from the city – and we duly returned the following Sunday to view what I hoped would be our future home.

Noreen, however, thought it was a complete dump, and nothing more ever came of it.

The 1940s were absolutely fascinating years. It was a period when you could go almost everywhere by train. There were fifty million miles of railway track in Ireland (although I may possibly be thinking of India here),* and in the days before cars were so numerous, it was the most popular mode of travel. You could even go places by train that you couldn't get to on foot. Thousands of small rural depots dotted the country, and I remember feeling a great sadness when they were all closed down over one weekend in 1962. Once, I took a train to Cobh, and stopped at over five hundred stations along the way. I knew for a time the stationmaster at Killetmore, County Carlow, Johnny Walsh. He had been in charge there for sixty years, and had never once seen a passenger alight on his platform. One American, in search of his roots in the early 1920s, got off, took a look around, and then got back on to the train immediately. No one quite understood why a station had been built in such a small place. Killetmore was so minuscule that no one knew where it was exactly, and there were grave doubts about whether it existed at all. Certainly, it wasn't to be found on any map.

I think of it now because I passed through it in 1948 with the then Managing Director of the Abbey Theatre, Ernest Blythe. He was a stern Northern Protestant, but had done his bit for Irish freedom during the Tan war.

* See note about Mother Theresa's face on page 106.

We were on our way south to collect stories of Irish folklore. This had become a bit of a hobby of mine, while Blythe was a great Irish-language enthusiast, and was always on the lookout for subject matter that would be of interest to the national theatre.

In Clonakilty, we stayed for a while at a house belonging to a man called Bunty Rafter. Blythe and Bunty had been friends for years, and the Rafter family were most welcoming to both of us. A very, very funny incident happened while we were there involving the family's pet rabbit, called Mickey. Blythe had taken a bath and, while he was relaxing in the warm water, Mickey had mischievously crept into his trousers. When Blythe stepped out of the tub and hitched his pants up, the wayward bunny found himself pressed into the Abbey supremo's groin. Somehow, he got his teeth into a very tender part of Blythe's anatomy, and wouldn't let go for all the tea in China. The only solution, Bunty insisted, was to shoot Mickey. I still remember the scene; Blythe with the trousers around his ankles, Mickey clinging on for dear life to his namesake, and Bunty aiming the shotgun at the rabbit's head. You can imagine the agitated state Blythe was in at this stage, as anything less than 100 per cent accuracy would result in carnage not seen since the Ballyseedy Mortar incident during the civil war. Happily, the rabbit was successfully dispatched, and the Man from the Abbey survived intact. The whole affair amused me for weeks. It was a genuinely hilarious incident, the like of which rarely happens nowadays.

The remainder of our journey was very successful in

terms of collecting folklore, though I only met Blythe once or twice subsequently.

As well as banning books, we also had fun in the Censorship Board banning plays. Although this was an area technically outside our remit, we could always bring anything we thought to be obscene to the attention of the authorities. In the spring of 1949, myself and Gloinn heard that there was a very dirty play showing in town by a new Northern Ireland playwright called Ranger MacWoods, rejoicing in the provocative title *Big Jugs*. It was the first time we were to come across this young man, but over the years he was to become something of a thorn in our side. The information which trickled down to us about *Big Jugs* seemed to suggest that the play was very 'near the knuckle' indeed. When we got a copy of the script, our worst fears were realized. I have dug up the original copy from my personal archive to remind myself just exactly what a piece of pure filth it was, and even by today's standards, when we have grown wearily used to the exploits of people like the footballer Paul Gascoigne, it still makes chilling reading. The highly unlikely scenario concerns a nun who has a child by an archbishop. The nun, at this time almost penniless, then becomes a belly dancer and a writer of pornographic novels. Her son grows up to be a homosexual, but is obsessed by fat men with folds of fat that remind him of women's breasts (the 'big jugs' of the title). He eventually catches up with the archbishop (a very large man) and forces him at gunpoint to perform an erotic striptease for his pleasure. The final item of clothing removed is a large bra which the archbishop wears on his chest as if he were a woman. The young man then masturbates over the bra in a scene that lasts for almost a quarter of the play's length. I think anyone would agree that this type of thing is completely unacceptable even in this overly permissive age, but how MacWoods thought he could get away with this in the Dublin theatre of the 1940s, I'll never know.

Needless to say, the play was closed down after three performances, and MacWoods slunk away to England for a time. However, he was to re-emerge three or four years later with his first novel, *Fill up me Johnnies*. Suffice to say, if you know what a 'johnny' is, then you know what substance one fills it up with. Unsurprisingly, this horrendous trash was immediately banned, and MacWoods was forced to sell his 'work' independently in bars around Dublin.

Around this period, I visited London for the first time. Myself and Gloinn had travelled over for a conference on Catholics and Sin (big subject!) and decided to spend a few days in what was then the capital of England. It was the first time I had left Ireland (Gloinn, as well as his visit to Germany, had been to Rome and Lourdes many times), and I was slightly apprehensive about the prospect. My brother Brian had emigrated shortly after the war, and lived with his Roscommon-born wife Betty in a small house in Cricklewood. (I call it a house, but it was little more than an outside wall made of bricks enclosing four or five rooms.) I visited them during our

My parents circa their wedding day. My mother is the woman on the left.

A treasured family heirloom: my father's mug commemorating the centenary of the 1798 rebellion. (*Photo copyright Eoin O'Ceallaigh, 2000*)

The serious, and not-so-serious (!) sides of Gloinn.

Two studies of Larry Hoey: at around the time of our first meeting at the 1932 Eucharistic Congress (back row, second right), and in later life, on a horse.

The Prayer Crusade

In preparation for the Eucharistic Congress a complete organising machine has been set up. Every aspect of the Congress will be examined in detail. Every problem incidental to the great gathering will be carefully studied. A vast amount of energy of mind and body will be expended. But all this merely human endeavour will have been wasted if the spiritual preparation for this greatest of human acts of homage is allowed to fall into abeyance.

Last May a Crusade of Prayer for the success of the Congress was inaugurated. On May 24th, the first lot of prayer leaflets was despatched from the Congress Office. Since then three quarters of a million have been sent out all over Ireland and to many parts of the English speaking world. Some have found their way to China, some to the Gold Coast; others to India. The great treasure of prayers and good works that these labourers in Christ's vineyard have laid in supplication before the throne of God may be judged from the following figures, which represent the various good works promised up to the end of October, 1930 :—

Masses	2,549,931
Holy Communions	1,926,166
Spiritual Communions	3,951,704
Benedictions	1,072,079
Stations of the Cross	390,752
Acts of Self-Denial	4,270,795
Visits to Blessed Sacrament	2,026,128
Eucharistic of Holy Hour	2,905,392
Alms	70,351
Little Office of the B.V.M.	463,465
Other Spiritual Acts	10,024,590

But the Thirty-first International Eucharistic Congress is not the concern of Ireland alone, nor yet of the English-speaking world alone. It is the concern of the Universal Church. Every race, every land, will join in it. It will be a supreme and world-wide act of homage to Christ. That it may be productive of the greatest good to the whole world and to the Church it is necessary that all should lend their aid. Supplies of the leaflets can be had from the Eucharistic Congress Office, 8 Lower Abbey Street, Dublin, price 4/6 per 1,000 ; 6d. per 100, plus postage outside Ireland and Great Britain.

An explanation of 'The Prayer Crusade', from the official Eucharistic Congress programme.

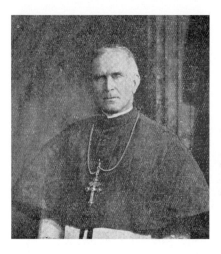

Cardinal MacRory. He surprised
me with his Al Jolson impression!

Our wedding day, 1933. The
happy bride and groom to the
right of picture.

Ernest Blythe. A funny incident involving a
rabbit almost ended in tragedy for the
Abbey Theatre supremo. (*Hulton Getty*)

Our dog 'Festy', who died when he licked fluid from Noreen's knee.

Above: Lourdes 1964. 'Ready for take-off!'

Below: Gloinn took this snap of me and Maire on the plane. Due to a double exposure, the 'ghost-like' figure of Father Joe Collins is also present! (Note: Maire's face was later scratched out by Gloinn after one of their many arguments)

Noreen was fascinated by these straws in a glass.

Eamon de Valera. (*Bert Hardy/Hulton Getty*)

Hitler. (*Hulton Getty*)

Gay Byrne. (*RTE Ireland*)

Pope John Paul II. (*Hulton Getty*)

trip, and was most amused to learn that a foreign family lived next door to them. While I was out with Brian in his small back garden looking at his lettuce, I heard some of these people having a conversation in their garden, and I must say I found the funny language in which they were talking to each other highly amusing. I hope they, at least, understood each other, because to me it sounded like a load of rubbish! I have always found foreigners, with their unusual skin colours, mad languages and ignorant customs absolutely hilarious, and I think it's a shame that in recent years it's become unfashionable to poke fun at them. I certainly don't think they themselves ever minded it.

London itself I thought was an odd type of a place. Brian expressed sorrow at being forced to live in a non-Catholic country, and I sympathized with his pain at being surrounded by loads of atheistic Protestants. At least he could express his identity through his involvement in Irish and Catholic societies, and showed me what must have been over a hundred of his membership cards. A very amusing misunderstanding occurred between us when he informed me that he had recently started work at a bomb-making factory in Camberwell. My immediate response was to express surprise that the British government were taking such a surprisingly open approach to activities of the Irish Republican Army. No, no, Brian responded, it was a bomb-making factory for the Royal Air Force! We both laughed at this simple misunderstanding until the tears were rolling down our cheeks. Gloinn returned home from evening mass to find us in this helpless state of hilarity, and thought the King must have been forced to abdicate after a sexual scandal.

Our visit to the 'UK' was memorable for two other incidents. Gloinn was bitten by a bat in the Tower of London and had to undergo a painful anti-tetanus injection in his groin, and we met the actor Jack Hawkins in a bookshop in Charing Cross Road. Hawkins was a real 'gent', and I felt sorry for him years afterwards when I heard he'd died.

Brian confided to me during our visit that he was not very happy working in the factory. Although the English people he worked with seemed nice enough, he was sure that when he left their company they immediately started making fun of him and began to imitate his accent. This, of course, happens to every Irish person who works in England. In recent years it has become rather uncomfortable to witness the spectacle of our current Taoiseach, Mr Ahern, sharing a platform with the British Prime Minister, Mr Blair, after one of their many meetings to keep the ill-thought-out, deeply unpopular and discredited Northern Ireland 'Peace Process' on the rails. One can tell from the television pictures that Mr Blair quite obviously feels superior, and looks down on our Taoiseach as some kind of brainless leprechaun. It is not hard to imagine, immediately after Mr Ahern has left 10 Downing Street, the Prime Minister laughing at him and mimicking his accent to the amusement of his colleagues in the New Labour party. This type of behaviour shows a marked lack of respect to our Taoiseach, and

prompted a letter of protest from me to the British embassy. Needless to say, I have yet to receive a reply, except for a letter from an official with a double-barrelled name informing me that any perceived lack of respect to the Taoiseach existed solely in my own mind.

Back in Ireland, it was a time of great activity for the League of the Mother of God against Sin. Accidentally, the new coalition government had installed a Communist, Dr Noel Browne, as Minister of Health, and he had pledged to institute 'State Health Care', a thinly disguised form of Soviet-style Socialism, which involved giving free milk to babies. The people were not fooled, and Gloinn, Larry and myself became very active in the fight to safeguard the family. As a result of our activities, *The Irish Press* did a long interview with Gloinn and myself in Gloinn's house in Clontarf. I remember Maire bringing in some tea and biscuits during the interview, and the sheer size of her obviously flabbergasted the young reporter (she must have been up to a 'personal best' of about thirty stone at the time). The hack spent much of his time in the subsequent interview describing her in unflattering detail, using terms such as 'grotesque', 'whale-like' and 'a massive lump of a woman whose every footstep shook the room like an earthquake'. Gloinn was mightily embarrassed by all this, and wouldn't talk to Maire for weeks afterwards. In the long term, Browne was forced out of office, the Bishops had their way, and sanity was restored to the country. It was a major victory for the League.

Although I cannot put an exact date on it, it must have been around this time that Noreen began to suffer from the numerous illnesses and afflictions that would torment her constantly until the merciful relief of her long-overdue death. I have already mentioned the considerable inconveniences and irritations that these caused me, and on more than one occasion I was forced to pray to God for an early release for my wife. Sadly, it was not to be, and her poor health would plague me for another thirty years. I remember her constantly complaining about a 'bad back' around the end of the 1940s, and a kind of stiffness in her joints. Although, as I have already mentioned, she did not suffer from the sheer laziness that was a major characteristic of Maire, my initial reaction was nonetheless the quite normal one of suspecting that she was attempting to 'dodge' housework. However, a visit to our local GP, Doctor Sweetman, confirmed that there was indeed 'something wrong with her'. Although he recommended a period of rest for Noreen, this was obviously unacceptable to me. To again quote Gloinn's enquiry concerning Mrs Benazir Bhutto's domestic situation: 'Who's going to make the dinner?' Well, there was only one person going to make the dinner in our house, and that was Noreen. I am not ashamed – in fact I am rather proud – that I have never washed a plate or fried a sausage in my life, and will always believe that this is a wife's remit. Gloinn and myself once spent a weekend together in a caravan in Kilkee, and his attempt to boil an egg led to a fire in which a local itinerant perished. Men have little talent for cookery, and I am both amazed and amused by the amount of male chefs we now see on our television screens. Most of them, of course, are completely useless at cooking, but absolute masters of self-promotion.

Noreen recovered from her initial back trouble after a week or two, but it was only a temporary break from the multitude of maladies that would put her 'out of service' over the coming decades. I remember once she suffered from a build up of fluid on her leg which required draining every day. This unpleasant task fell to me when Noreen was unable (or more likely, unwilling) to undergo the procedure herself. Her leg initially 'blew up' just before an annual conference on euthanasia which Gloinn and I were due to attend in Galway. This conference was always great fun, and I was certainly not going to let my wife's incapacitation keep me away from it. (Although, because of Church teaching, I was opposed to euthanasia, on more than one occasion I was willing to make an exception for Noreen!) At that time we had a dog called Festy, and I managed to fix up an apparatus whereby the hound could lick the fluid off Noreen's leg while I was away. Such was the 'crack' at the euthanasia conference, that I returned home three days later than expected. I was met at the door by Lorcan, who told me that during my absence the leg had started haemorrhaging badly (more ill luck) and that Festy had drunk so much of the escaping fluid that he'd died. Meanwhile, Mammy was in hospital staring at the prospect of amputation. In the end, she managed to hold on to the leg, but I was very annoyed at her for causing such unnecessary disruption.

Many years later, I met the late, great Mother Theresa of Calcutta in Rome at a fundraising darts tournament. I happened to mention Noreen's problems to the legendary blue and white striped poverty mogul, and enquired about the prospect of shipping her out to India to be cared for by Mother Theresa's nuns. Her reply to me was rather long-winded and relayed to me in barely decipherable pidgin English. I admit that after a while I became so bored that I started counting the lines on the face of the pint-sized crone. (A number roughly equivalent to the amount in miles of Indian railway track, I remember thinking!) Anyway, nothing became of it, and Noreen remained in Ireland for the rest of her life.

Gloinn once painted a beautiful portrait of Mother Theresa, who was very much a heroine to both of us. He has dabbled fitfully in painting over the years, and while he is not a highly skilled technician, he works with great energy and enthusiasm. Since his semi-retirement, he has painted many scenes of the countryside near his cottage in Connemara. In his later years, he has preferred landscape painting, but both Noreen and myself sat for him many times in the past to test his skills of portraiture. He has never attempted a picture of Maire. He says, jokingly, that he would never find a canvas big enough, but we both know that the pain of looking at his wife for the period required to produce a picture would be too much to bear. The inflated shape of her form, the thick and unruly eyebrows – in fact, one large eyebrow where two eyebrows have merged – the lank hair, the pockmarked skin, the oversized and ill-matched 'cauliflower' ears that look like they belong to two different heavyweight boxers; to dwell on such bodily squalor for too long would break any man's spirit. To realize that one was actually married to this wreck, well . . .

The picture of Mother Theresa hung in Gloinn's pantry for many years. Like all talented painters, Gloinn knows the importance of getting a good 'likeness' in a portrait, and his rendition of the old lady was just great. Her eyes didn't so much follow you around the room as chase you out the door and pursue you for several miles up the road. His preferred medium was poster paints on paper, and during the mid 1970s he did a special deal where he would get cheap paint used in primary schools from the Department of Education. He always felt that oil paints were too expensive and took too long to dry.

A man who bestrode the Ireland of much of this century like some kind of giant, oversized colossus was the Archbishop of Dublin, Doctor John Charles McQuaid, who Gloinn and I knew extremely well. On one occasion he even said to us (whilst, very untypically, smiling bashfully and looking at the ground) that we were his best friends outside the Church. We were obviously very thrilled indeed at this affectionate expression of intimacy. I remember vividly one occasion in 1944 when we brought a risqué cartoon in the satirical magazine *Dublin Opinion* to his attention on the very day the Allied troops landed on the beaches of Normandy. We thought the drawing was immoral as it showed a couple kissing, not outdoors on a street, as is acceptable during early days of courtship, but inside a house. On closer inspection, Gloinn noticed that the lady in the cartoon did not have a wedding ring on her finger. A trip to the archbishop was duly pencilled in.

Doctor McQuaid greeted us warmly in his palatial living room, which was filled with leopard-skin rugs, busts from ancient Rome, hunting trophies, original masterpieces by Titian and Vermeer, and signed photographs of Mussolini, Franco, and various Hollywood film stars. He did not yet have an autographed picture of Hitler, but was expecting one by return of post – although he feared that 'Adolf' (I was impressed that they seemed to be on first-name terms) might be preoccupied with other matters. He studied the cartoon for some time, and while he felt it was mild ('compared to some of the stuff that I have to deal with!'), he agreed with us that a child could misinterpret it as giving the 'thumbs up' to cohabitation outside of wedlock. I remember him perusing the evidence carefully, his half-glasses (always the sign of an intellectual mind) perched on his long nose. It came as no surprise that an apology was printed in the following edition of *Dublin Opinion.*

There were many times over the years when we visited him to draw his attention to some lewd or immoral conduct, or material which, despite his renowned vigilance, may have escaped his notice. I remember once Gloinn had received a calendar through the post from his local parish church in Clontarf. A list of holy days of obligation was crammed into the corner of the calendar beside 'July', and due to lack of space, possibly caused by the year in question being a leap year and having an extra day in February, 'The Feast of the Immaculate Conception' became abbreviated to 'The Feast of Immac. Conception'. Immac, of course, was a popular product used to stop hair growing out of women's legs. It may have been an innocent enough mistake, but it was also an error which could easily cause offence to many parishioners. On the intervention of Doctor McQuaid, the calendar was withdrawn shortly afterwards.

The Archbishop always greeted us with great courtesy, and listened to our concerns with patience; usually resolving to 'deal with the problem'. On one occasion, I got the distinct impression that Doctor McQuaid would have been willing to resort to very extreme measures after we brought to his attention a documentary on RTE television about illegitimacy. Noting the name of the producer of the programme, he peered over his spectacles and remarked wearily to myself and Gloinn, 'Ah, yes, I've had trouble with this fellow before.' He then began to mutter that there was such a thing as a just war and that often people have to die in order for the greater good to triumph. He also used terms such as 'rub them out' and seemed to be familiar with aspects of machine gunning. Later, myself and Gloinn both agreed that the Archbishop must have been a big fan of the American television programme *The Untouchables*. I may have misinterpreted these dark mumblings, and I would never suggest that Doctor McQuaid would have sanctioned the actual murder of RTE producers, but I remember being slightly puzzled at the time. Gloinn was 'dying for a drink' after the meeting, so we went to the nearest pub to the Archbishop's residence. Several whiskeys later, Gloinn suddenly said to me, 'You don't think he wants us to kill him?', referring to the producer. I assured my old friend that we should leave the whole affair for the time being, and to await further instructions from the Boss. Needless to say, nothing more became of the matter, and the next time we called in to see the Archbishop, he never mentioned the RTE man.

However, a week or two afterwards, Gloinn wrote a typically forthright piece in the official newspaper of the League of the Mother of God, *The Clarion Call*, expressing his own thoughts on how far one should go in preserving the moral fabric of society. The article was vintage McTire, fearlessly striking out at the liberals and heathens in no uncertain terms. A few days later, the house of a Protestant senator mentioned in the article was firebombed (an incident which recalled for me the heady days of 1920–1923), and Gloinn was subsequently arrested. Luckily, he had an alibi (he had been to Lough Mullet with Maire and Larry) and was eventually released a few days before Christmas 1949. However, he later told me that he had paid local hooligans ten pounds to carry out the attack.

Thus ended another decade. While most of Europe had been ravaged by war, Ireland had taken no part in the conflict, and while people elsewhere recall it as a time of horror, death and loss, I remember it mostly for Noreen's back pains.

A poet once wrote that one could never guess what was going to happen in the future, and that was certainly true about the next decade. No one knew what was going to occur, and when things did happen, largely they were unexpected.

CHAPTER 6

Hurrying Through the Threshold

The 1950s were a very exciting time in Ireland. Censorship remained strict, government, by whatever party, was deeply conservative, and the country remained largely an agricultural and rural-based society controlled by the Church. All this was terrific, but sadly, by the end of the decade, our little island would become increasingly tarnished by the wider world and beyond. It was a time of colour films, Elvis Presley and an increase in illegitimate births. All three, of course, were linked. Technicolor films such as *Ben Hur* and *Oklahoma!* led many Irish people to believe that life was a lot more exciting than it actually was, while Presley's music quite simply drove them mad. I imagine the shock that the first monkey experienced when he was launched into space would be an accurate comparison to what Gloinn went through when he first saw *High Society*. (I also suspect that the facial expression would be somewhat similar!) I remember many poor wretches emerging from picture houses around the country in an agitated state, as they had seen colours, such as bright blues and yellows, that they would never come across in their own dismal lives. How could someone, for example, emerging from a dazzling 'swords and sandals' epic, showing at their local picture house in Longford, be expected to deal with the dissimilarity between the Hollywood vision of life and the grim reality of their own lot in Ballinalee or Carrickboy? God help them, I used to think. I was under no illusions. Ireland was more suited to (a low-contrast) black and white. Presley's music I found more of an irritant, though amongst younger people it caused sexual desire and a lack of respect for authority. My own children, thankfully, never went for it, and were much fonder of slow ballads in an Irish vein.

By 1950, I was probably the best semi-professional poet in Ireland. In March that year, I was awaiting publication of my sixth book, *Hochaid Na Bliaroid Glas* (*Stroking the Bleary Grass*), and had been invited to speak at a Literary Festival in Kilkenny, something which I was very much looking forward to. But some very bizarre and inexplicable incidents were to take place before I would reach my destination. I set out on March 18th, coincidentally the day after St Patrick's Day, suspecting nothing of the strange sequence of events that were about to occur. I had my hair cut especially for the occasion (not in an unusual style; just neatly trimmed), and had splashed out on a suitably 'literary-looking' check writer's jacket and bow tie. I was driving through the dark night, mildly concerned that by wearing a bow tie I might be mistaken for a Protestant (or a surgeon!), when, just outside Tullow, I suddenly saw a very bright light in the sky. Then, a circular craft, the shape of a large saucer, descended in front of me on the road and I blacked out. The next thing I remember is being stripped naked by long, thin, green creatures with oval-shaped heads. After this initial 'preparation', I recall, very hazily, a series of weird experiments being carried out on me which caused some discomfort in the anal area. (I had this checked out later in hospital, and was alarmed to learn that some minor damage had been caused, probably as a result of a large object being inserted. To my great embarrassment, the young doctor asked, in a rather cheeky and over-familiar fashion, if I had 'been getting up to something with the wife?' He obviously didn't know Noreen.)

I thought nothing more of my experiences until I saw a documentary programme about something called 'alien abduction' on television last year. A healthily tanned man called Hector in a short-sleeved white shirt from New Mexico was describing a very similar experience to my own. I wondered if I had been a victim of abduction by extraterrestrial beings on that night many years ago. Nothing unusual like that had happened to me before, except for the time when God spoke to me while I was filling up my car with petrol at a garage in Athboy. (Thankfully, it wasn't anything important. Unlike other unfortunates whom God has spoken to, he didn't actually ask me to do anything. He just said a basic 'well done, keep up the good work'.) But even that wasn't so strange, because according to Catholic teaching, God exists whereas aliens obviously don't. I talked it over with Noreen and we agreed that, whatever way one looked at it, something out of the ordinary had happened. I was intrigued as to why Martians, or whatever they were, would decide to land just outside Tullow. (Noreen said that, judging by the look of some of the locals, they might have had relations there! This was a very funny remark, one of only two she made in almost fifty years of marriage.) Gloinn once mentioned to me that he had also had a similar 'close encounter', although in his case I suspected it was most likely a delusion caused by drink. Over the years, many other people have confided in me, claiming to have been the hapless victims of abductions by creatures from distant planets. This list includes our old friend Archbishop John Charles McQuaid, ex-presidential candidate Brian Lenihan, former jockey Pat Taafe (best known for his tremendous achievements on that fine steeplechaser 'Arkle'), and an Irish broadcaster and quiz-show host, well known in Britain, whom I shall not name lest it might harm his career. Doctor McQuaid in particular was very puzzled by his ordeal. He told me that while he was going through his experiences at the hands of the aliens, after being 'captured' while saying a novena in the grounds of Blackrock College, he had for the only time in his life begun to foster some doubts about his vocation. During a pause in the proceedings, as the mysterious space people were preparing him for an enema, the Archbishop asked where the Church fitted into all this, but they either deliberately ignored him, or were so focused on the complicated manoeuvre about to be attempted that they failed to notice his interruption. It's all most peculiar. If these creatures do exist, then is God aware of them? If He is, I sincerely hope that He is controlling them. The other possibility – that they are controlling God – doesn't bear thinking about. It could also be the case that there is someone else controlling both God and the aliens, but that I regard as the least likely scenario. (Although it would make a fascinating subject for a film by Steven Spielberg!) Gloinn's thoughts were very focused on these matters immediately after his alleged abduction, and combined with his generous intake of alcohol, eventually led to what nowadays we would call a 'nervous breakdown'. It was a trying time for him and Maire, but he made a full recovery in due course.

The early 1950s were, on the whole, a difficult period for Gloinn. Typical of his misfortune was the occasion when he was arrested after an incident in a car early one morning in Baggot Street. At first he denied the allegations, but at least fifteen people on the top deck of a bus saw him with the 'lad' out of his trousers, and he eventually admitted the offence. Even today, he becomes embarrassed when the topic arises in conversation, which it often does – usually at my instigation! He admitted to me privately afterwards that it had been some years since Maire and himself had conjugated, and the frustration was driving him mad. Tragically, it all came out, literally, that one morning in a busy Dublin street. Poor Gloinn has always been in a difficult position regarding his sex life. As her husband, he certainly had every right to expect sexual favours from Maire, but he was, at the same time, quite understandably, repelled at the thought of going anywhere near her. On their honeymoon he tried 'every trick in the book' to excite himself before the inaugural conjugal experience, but in the deadening presence of Maire he was unable to rise to the occasion. As a result, his wife remained a virgin for several years after their marriage. She was only finally deflowered while Gloinn was suffering from unusual hormonal side effects while on tablets for depression. He confided to me that this first full-on sexual adventure was 'horrendous', and he spent most of the next three months on a spiritual retreat in Waterford as a result. It says much about Maire's unfailing ability to dampen sexual desire in her husband* when one learns that Gloinn has, according to himself, a *'monumental'* sex drive (something, thanks be to God, which has never been a problem for me). Noreen and myself would often notice a discoloration on the carpet in the front room of Gloinn's house in front of the television set during the early 1970s, a time when very explicit drama series were being aired on the British TV channels. He once told me that he 'loved sex' and couldn't stop thinking about it all the time. Crippling images of the tawdriest nature would leap into his head at all hours of the day and night and torment him so much that he even considered exorcism. I read somewhere that the American actor Michael Douglas (son of Hollywood legend Kirk) is of a similar mind to Gloinn, and admits to being 'addicted

---

* Gloinn said to me once that Maire could have solved the problem of vice in Soho in the 1970s by just walking around the area. The sight of her would have put any potential punter off sex for life!

to riding'. A major difference between the two men, however, is that Douglas is a big movie star living in Hollywood surrounded by beautiful women, while Gloinn has no outlet for his unfortunate urges except relieving himself in cars or, even worse, in Maire. In recent years, his desperate remedy has been to gain relief using two cushions, Fairy Liquid, and a thin plastic bag used to transport tomatoes. He confessed this to me when he was very drunk, and this image of my old friend, ninety-something years old, grunting and groaning and thrusting into his old sofa, while he concentrates on an image of Sophia Loren – he's always had a 'soft spot' for Sophia – in a copy of *OK* magazine propped up before him, causes me nothing but pain. (This type of activity is also, of course, under Catholic law, highly illegal.) He also told me that due to his great age, he is often there for an hour or more before he can get a 'result'. In a bid to cheer him up, I told him that if he can get any 'result' at all at his age, he's doing well. I know that he sees my lack of any recognizable sexual appetite as a great blessing, and he reminded me recently of something that I had said just after I started going out with Noreen that amused him. Apparently, my remark was, 'I'm uncomfortable enough in my own body let alone someone else's!' (I must admit, I laughed along heartily with Gloinn when he reminded me of it.)

An extraordinary and inexplicable event occurred in 1952 when Maire left him briefly for another man. Many years before she had discovered that she would never be able to have children because she was too fat, and

Gloinn told me that they were having a furious argument about this when she suddenly stormed out of the house and up the road. He also said that he had inadvertently called her 'Damp Squib'* – a nickname I had suggested around the time of their marriage which Gloinn thought hilarious – and this had made her even angrier. Thankfully, her infidelity lasted only a short time, and before too long she returned to the family unit. She has never told anyone (or at least neither Gloinn nor myself) who this Romeo was, and it has caused endless speculation amongst us. Who on God's earth would fancy Maire? Someone, certainly, whose senses had been considerably blunted to the extent that they must have been more or less redundant. Frankenstein's monster would perhaps come closest to fitting the bill. (I may not yet have mentioned Maire's constant hacking cough or her unique body odour. 'She stinks to high heaven!' Gloinn would often exclaim in despair.) In the end, the McTire marriage has lasted for more than sixty years, and I have often thought that it was a victory for stoicism over romance, and for loyalty over personal happiness. It has survived alcoholism, boredom, lovelessness, sexual frustration, suicide attempts and mental and physical illness to become what it is today: a strong and persuasive argument against divorce.

On the television recently, I saw an American entertainer called Ru Paul. This woman was unusually tall, and I

* Gloinn usually shortens this to 'The Squib', as in 'I had an awful row with The Squib last night.'

immediately knew there was something wrong with her. Sure enough, she turned out to be a man. Whenever I see crazy people like Ms/Mr Paul, with their alternative life-styles, permissive attitudes towards sex, and be-ribboned white poodles, I often think of Larry Hoey. What would Larry and Ru Paul talk about if they ever met? How *would* they get on? It is endlessly fascinating to contrast such different personalities. My guess is that Larry would say little (from what I have seen of him/her, Ms/Mr Paul tends to 'hog' the conversation), but he would not be impolite or hostile. Rather, at the end of the day, in his own gentle way, he would say a little prayer to God, asking Him to eliminate people like Ms/Mr Paul from the planet. I would guess that, unlike Larry, prayer, confession and mass going feature little in the life of Ms/Mr Paul. She/he doubtless has other concerns to occupy her/his thoughts. Probably God has created people like Ru Paul deliberately, in order to illustrate in even sharper contrast the goodness and spiri-tuality of the Larry Hoeys of this world. As a Jesuit friend of mine, Father Reynard Floody, once said to me about God, 'there's method in His madness'.

In the spring of 1951, myself, Larry and Gloinn shared an unforgettable experience together. It contained drama, danger, tragedy and triumph in equal measure, and we were lucky to live to tell the tale. The previous September, I had entered a competition in *The Catholic Brain*, a short-lived (one issue) publication which I had founded earlier that year with the actor Jimmy O'Dea.

Luckily, and after much effort, I had secured an all-expenses trip to Rio de Janeiro (courtesy of our friend and patron Archbishop McQuaid) for the celebrations for the beatification of some Brazilian nun as the top prize in our inaugural readers' competition. Naturally, and to encourage as many entries as possible, members of *The Catholic Brain* staff were allowed to take part in the contest. The staff at this time consisted of myself, Gloinn and Larry (Jimmy O'Dea had recently left the magazine after a row over who should pay for bus fares to editorial meetings). The contestants were asked to answer one question (very easy – 'name the last ten popes') and the correct entries were placed in Larry's trilby hat for the 'grand prize draw'. Imagine my surprise and delight when, after several false starts, Gloinn drew out my own name. It was a near-miraculous occurrence, and presented me with an opportunity that I was very much looking forward to grasping, literally, with both hands. My travelling companions were to be, of course, Larry and Gloinn. It seemed fitting that I should share my good fortune with the witnesses of my success.

We set out first by ship for New York, from where we would fly on to South America. When we arrived in the 'Big Stable', we were amazed at the sheer bloody size of the place. And the skyscrapers! We couldn't wait to get to the top of the Empire State Building, visit the Statue of Liberty, and take in all the other sights that we'd only ever seen in films. Again, as in London, all the differently coloured people gave us a great laugh. 'Look at those lads!' shouted Larry, pointing at a group of Japanese labourers on Second Avenue. I honestly thought the excitement was going to kill him.

Gloinn got terribly drunk the first night we were there, and had an altercation with a Puerto Rican gang. If you have seen the musical film *West Side Story*, you'll know that these boyos can be ferocious if provoked, and I'm afraid that Gloinn goaded them terribly. It all started in a bar in Manhattan, where Gloinn dragged me to after we'd been to see the rather grandiose tomb of General Ulysses S. Grant. A few of these Puerto Ricans were playing pool nearby, and Gloinn started coming out with some typical drunk talk: 'Oh, the Irish are the top dogs in New York', 'America wouldn't be the country it is if the Irish hadn't come over', all that kind of stuff. Then he began to use what would nowadays be called 'politically incorrect' terms to describe some of the Hispanics present. Anyway, eventually they had enough of it, and gave poor Gloinn a terrible kicking. The next morning, more than his head was sore.

After a lot of travelling, we ended up in Peru. At this stage, due to me losing my passport, Gloinn's heavy drinking, and Larry being suddenly struck down with a dizzy bout of diarrhoea, our journey was becoming something of a nightmare. Eventually, due to more mix-ups, we ended up having to charter a plane to Rio, in order that we wouldn't be late for the beatification. Larry, particularly, did not want to miss even one second of this event. He had never seen anybody being turned into a saint before, and he simply could not wait to throw himself into an orgy of mass-going, confession-making and prayer marathons in a city dominated by a statue of the founder of Catholicism. ('Look at that big Jesus,' Larry said when he first saw a postcard featuring the statue.) After some negotiations, we managed to hire a small plane, and it turned out that we were to be accompanied on our journey by the Archbishop of Lima, Doctor Carlos Zanzibar. Our hearts sank somewhat when we saw the aircraft, a tiny crate that seemed to have bullet holes in the cockpit and wing tips, no doubt a sad legacy of some high-spirited dispute (over a woman?) which so bedevils the peoples of South America. Our worst fears were soon realized when, high over the Andes, the engine of the craft started to splutter, and we began to fear for our lives. I remember an acute physical pain in my stomach, such was the intense feeling of dread. It was a sensation which I would not experience again until many years later when I first saw Sinead O'Connor on television. Larry started spouting Hail Marys, Gloinn headed for the whiskey bottle and the Archbishop began shrieking incoherently in his native tongue. Larry's diarrhoea also went into overdrive, and it may have been this, as much as the prospect of imminent death, which forced the pilot to jump from the plane, taking with him the one available parachute. It looked like our 'number was up', and I prepared myself for death by praying silently. Then there was a loud 'bang' and everything went black.

When I came round, the first thing I was aware of was the freezing cold. It was also very dark, and I could hear

a howling wind. Was I in Monaghan?!!!* As conscious-
ness dawned on me, I slowly remembered my true pre-
dicament. I then realized that I had been lucky enough
to survive the crash, and when I tried to move the
different parts of my body, I noted with relief that
everything seemed to be in working order. (No, I didn't
try *all* of them!) I was aware of the sound of moaning
coming from somewhere, and after a quick look around
I spotted the curled-up body of Gloinn lying about six
feet away, next to a gaping hole in the fuselage. 'Gloinn,'
I cried, 'are you all right?' 'Yes, Eoin,' he replied, 'I'm
grand, but I have an awful sore head on me.' He was
more bothered by his hangover than the plane crash!
Larry had, thankfully, also survived; something he
immediately put down to the intervention of the
Almighty. Unfortunately, the Archbishop of Lima had
not been so lucky, and we could see his lifeless body
lying near the wing tip which had unfortunately sliced
the top of his head off, revealing part of his brain. After
the initial feelings of relief that we had survived, we
became anxious about our chances of making it back to
civilization. We could only hope that someone would
realize what had happened to us and would come to the
rescue before we could die of hunger and exposure. But
after a few days, we began to fear the worst. The fuselage
of the wrecked aircraft offered some shelter from the

---

* A good-humoured joke aimed at my good friend, Father Ultan
Dwyer, who has been parish priest at several locations in
Monaghan for many years, and rarely stops complaining about
the cold!

harsh weather outside, but the food, and, in Gloinn's case, more importantly, the whiskey, had run out. Larry passed the time by doing something he had always wanted to do but never had the time: saying a mass backwards in Latin. I composed a few poems in my head, and Gloinn mostly slept, in between making notes for a possible film script of our adventure. But soon the food shortage proved to be a huge problem. We were thus faced with a dilemma almost too hideous to contemplate; should we eat the Archbishop?

We were able to put the problem on hold for another couple of days, but by that time the sheer hunger forced us to make a decision one way or the other. What should we do? One does not take a step into cannibalism lightly, especially when a member of the Hierarchy is involved. A lively debate ensued. Larry was very much against eating the Archbishop, Gloinn very much in favour. I was undecided. Gloinn stressed, in his summing-up, that we would not have to eat all of the Archbishop, just some of him, and certainly no parts that under Catholic teaching would be regarded as controversial. (I presume he meant the sexual organs. This was certainly a non-starter for me; in every sense of the word!)* Larry was adamant that in no circumstances would he eat any part of Doctor Zanzibar at all, even if he proved to be particularly tasty. Thankfully, and I am still grateful to God to this very day for the occurrence, we did not in the end have to make the choice. To our immense relief, we were

* The joke here is that the opening course of a meal is usually referred to as a 'starter'.

delivered from our peril by a mountain rescue team (complete with mules) just as we were putting things to a vote.

After a spell in hospital, where we each received telegrams from the Taoiseach, we returned home, shaken, certainly, but relatively unharmed by our ordeal. Archbishop Zanzibar received a state funeral in Lima.

The 1950s contained two years that were very important for Catholics; 1950 and 1954. 1950 was designated a Holy Year, and for the first time in Ireland, mass-going surpassed the magical 100 per cent mark. We wondered at the time why the Vatican had decided that 1950 would be particularly holy. Would it be holier than other years such as, for instance, 1572 or 1897? Towards the end of 1950, Larry in particular became very depressed at the thought of 1951 not being as holy as the previous twelve months, but then decided that in his own mind he would make the following years as holy as possible, without, of course, undermining the Church's position by making them any more holy than 1950.

1954 was Marian Year, celebrating the greatness of the Blessed Virgin Mary; very much the 'first lady' of Catholicism. Nearly every girl in Ireland born that year was christened Marian. Parents who were unable to call their child the name because an older daughter had already been given it, often re-christened the elder girl or named the new baby something that sounded similar. Recently I met two middle-aged ladies called 'Harian' Dowdall and 'Larian' Kelly.

As I have mentioned, Gloinn was for a short time a Member of Parliament in Dail Eireann. In 1954 he received the mandate from the voters of Laois/Offaly, and he takes immense pride in the fact that the people had such confidence in his abilities that they chose him as their representative in the temple of democracy that is Dail Eireann, possibly the greatest and most famous political institution in the world. He was, of course, elected on the Fianna Fail ticket. By the early 1950s we had both been toying with the idea of becoming party members for some years. I remember that I agreed with Gloinn at the time that de Valera was not quite forceful enough on the Northern Ireland issue, and this had been rather an obstacle for both of us. Gloinn's ideal solution to the 'Northern question' would have been a 'blitzkrieg' assault on the six counties from the south, based on Hitler's (him again!) lightning attack on Poland in 1939. I argued with Gloinn that this was largely impractical, as the Irish army didn't have any tanks. Faced with bald facts, Gloinn often becomes obstinate and is inclined to go into a deep sulk. This time was no different, and after an hour or two of stony silence as I explained the reality of the situation, he began cursing and bemoaning our lack of tanks. He even suggested that we could make a few tanks our-selves by hammering pieces of galvanized sheeting from sheds on to cars. While this fitted the definition of an (admittedly crude) armoured vehicle, it still was in no way a 'tank'. I also remember discussing the impracti-calities of driving along the notoriously bad roads on the southern side of the border, which we both agreed actual proper tanks would have difficulty in negotiating, such was their parlous state. ('Even the potholes have potholes!' I remember my cousin Jimmy Phillips saying to me once on a visit to Cavan as we rattled along the road to Belturbet.) However, Gloinn was confident that once we were on the northern side of the border, the far superior roads, symbolic of the much more prosperous Northern statelet, would speed us on our way. Our push on Belfast could be completed in twenty minutes, and the surly Unionists would immediately succumb. At this stage, I think the doorbell rang, Gloinn went to answer it, it turned out to be a priest he hadn't seen in years and the idea never surfaced again.

While Fianna Fáil had gone rather soft on the national issue, there was still much to admire in the 'soldiers of density'. De Valera was an arch conservative who made no secret of the fact that an unthinking devotion to religion should be the main concern in an Irishman's life. He had governed the country in accordance with his own deeply held religious convictions and had quite rightly prioritized the building of churches at the expense of food production, industry, or any kind of prosperity. He had seen that material wealth in other countries had invariably led to the spread of atheism, and was determined that this would not happen in Ireland. A Fianna Fáil election poster from the 1948 general election, under the heading 'Which Irishman Are You?', showed two drawings; a man dressed in an old overcoat sitting on a rickety chair staring into a fire and clutching a jam-jar filled with buttermilk, and a 'toff' in a fur coat driving a Rolls-Royce. A closer examination of the drawings showed that the man in front of the fire was smiling and the toff was not. The message was clear; it was better to sit on a rickety chair drinking buttermilk, knowing that you were going to Heaven, than to drive around in a posh car, knowing you were going to Hell. The slogan at the bottom said, quite simply, 'Vote de Valera'.

I remember joining Gloinn on the hustings outside Dillon's Hotel in Castleleonard on a freezing March day as the great campaign began. While he expected little opposition from his Fine Gael opponent, he would still have to put in a lot of hard work to woo the people of Laois/Offaly, a notoriously 'hard to please' lot who, on the whole, didn't give a damn about politics. An independent candidate, Father Austin Furney, a Republican Paedophile Priest, was expected to poll strongly and provide the main threat to Fianna Fail. Father Furney, whose father, mother, three uncles, an aunt and even the family dog (admittedly under protest) had died on Sinn Fein hunger strikes in the 1920s, had put himself forward in response to the execution of Jimmy Lamb, an IRA man who had shot a policeman during an incident at the All-Ireland Ploughing Championships. At that time, paedophilia was little understood either by the media or the public, and was not regarded as a handicap for a prospective member of parliament. In fact, there was once talk of forming a Paedophile Party, such was its popularity in the country.

The phenomenon of the Republican Paedophile Priest has been in Ireland for years. It is a grand old tradition which dates back many centuries. Father Osbert Gill, an RPP who fought at New Ross in 1798, wrote in his journal, after he had spent the day instructing the local peasantry in the use of pikes: 'Brave and bould lads one and all. Uniforms do not exist for our fine little ragged army, and the day was so warm that after Mass I drilled the boys from Arklow and Enniscorthy in the nuddy *[this either refers to a drill where all the men were in the nude, or the River Nuddy, a tributary of the Suir – E O'C]*. In the evening, we lit fires and cursed the Redcoats. All the talk is of when the French will land. After a supper of snipe and broken carrots, a boy, Naughton, from Bunclody, stayed awhile beneath my quilt and was my opponent in close quarter combat.'

A Regiment of Republican Paedophile Priests was raised in the Union army during the American Civil War, and was involved in a skirmish with Confederate Arse Bandits at the second battle of Bull Run. At the funeral of the old Fenian Jeremiah O'Donovan Rossa in 1915, the concelebrated mass was performed by RPPs from Ireland, the US, Britain and Australia. With the growing awareness and distrust of both priests and paedophilia, the phenomenon has died out in recent years, but one still reads in the news of occasional enthusiasts. Father Barry Hourican, a dear friend of both myself and Gloinn, revived the tradition by making the headlines in early 1998, and we shall come to his story later.

Gloinn was very confident that he could win the Dail seat, and felt he was getting a 'good reaction on the doorsteps'. I accompanied him on his many jaunts around the small farms of the midlands and was much struck by the poverty still apparent in rural Ireland. Jobs were few, and I read somewhere recently that the number-one occupation for men in the country during those years was clearing up after storms: a task which might earn them enough pennies for a pint or two down the pub to ease the misery. Many of the houses had no doors, windows or walls, and were often without roofs. The tops of the heads of members of families lucky enough to have walls could often be seen sticking over the structure as we approached the house up the narrow laneways.

Women then were not much interested in politics (oh happy days!) and wisely decided to leave the electoral choice to the man of the house, who was seldom able to come to the door, either because he was out in the fields or because he was incapacitated by drink. A cup of tea and perhaps a biscuit or two was always offered to us in houses which were 'traditionally Fianna Fail', and I was impressed and humbled by the generosity of the ignorant people that we met. Emigration to England increased in the 1950s, and often I noted that when we were talking to several members of the family, a number of them would suddenly emigrate halfway through the conversation – or even, as happened on more than one occasion – halfway through a sentence. Once, we entered a small farmhouse and happened upon a group of nine or ten persons. By the time we left, twenty minutes later, only the mother and the youngest two children were still living at home. The rest had set off to catch the boat to Holyhead. The subject of emigration was often raised by the people we met, and they were always impressed by Gloinn's solution to the problem: he would say a special prayer for them at night. Sure enough, when we returned to Dillon's Hotel one particular evening, I heard through the thin walls Gloinn's touching reminder to God of the poor emigrant's plight. Amongst his always moving remembrance of his own parents, he reminded God that He had a responsibility to look after the thousands of Irish Catholics leaving home every day: 'God bless Mammy and Daddy and don't forget the lonely emigrant too.' I don't think any man could have done more for the many millions who left the country during those harsh economic times.

Often on our travels we met people who were unsure as to the exact duties of a TD, or even what it meant. ('Teachtai Dala': 'Member of Parliament' in Irish.) One old man, I remember, rather misunderstood what Gloinn's role would be if elected. He seemed to believe that if Gloinn became a member of the Dail, he would assume supernatural powers and, amongst other skills, be able to turn water into wine. When Gloinn informed him this would not be the case, he said that he would vote for another candidate who 'would be able to do it'. (I heard afterwards that Paddy Harkey, the Fine Gael hopeful, had promised the old man that he 'could do that for him', a rather stark illustration of how far a politician will go to get votes.)

On the night of the count, always a tense time for politicians, Gloinn was elected by the narrowest margin possible: one vote. As usual when the result is as close as this, there were recounts, accusations, counter accusations, and dark mutterings of boxes of votes being tampered with. In fact, as we drove off to a local pub to celebrate that night, I noticed a large black ballot box in the back of Gloinn's car marked with the name 'Carrickowen', a particularly strong Fine Gael part of the constituency. I don't know what it was doing there, and I never asked. We were content to celebrate our good luck, and Gloinn that night was as drunk as I've ever seen him.

As I've mentioned, Gloinn's time in Dail Eireann was a relatively brief one. A general election was called only a couple of months after he took his seat and he had barely settled into the role of public representative before he was unceremoniously ousted. He had foolishly agreed to allow a cache of IRA arms to be lodged in the living room of his home (I advised him that he should at least hide them in a cellar or loft), which were intended to be used in the imminent border-bombing campaign of the period, and when he was raided after a tip-off to the Gardai, his only excuse was that they were a present from Maire and he didn't know much about it. The paradox of Fianna Fail's fierce, unswerving commitment to unification, while at same time being unwilling to lift a finger to actually bring it about was again starkly exposed, and Gloinn became an unfortunate victim of the situation. Dev himself broke the news to him in his office in Dail Eireann. It was yet another irony that as Gloinn was receiving a stern lecture from the Chief, on the wall behind him was a photograph of Dev, taken in his own living room in 1923, posing beside a stack of machine guns. It says a lot for Gloinn's loyalty to the old man that he never felt bitter over the incident and remained a Fianna Failer throughout the following years. Recently we watched together an old newsreel of Dev inspecting some volunteers in Connemara during the War of Independence. We noticed the impressive rows and rows of men that seemed to stretch for several miles into the distance. 'Look at the amount of fellows there,' Gloinn remarked. 'Wasn't Dev a great man to have so many followers?' It was only afterwards when I watched the video again that I noticed that the 'volunteers' in the background were actually stone walls. But Gloinn's point was still valid. And even if walls could have made political choices, I am sure they would have followed de Valera.

Before he was forced to put the brakes on his Republicanism, Gloinn's time in parliament, though short, was fruitful. He procured for me a job in the Department of Welfare that increased my salary by a thousand pounds a year, and he himself was able to enjoy many free gifts and perks from individuals, companies and firms in return for vague promises to the effect that he would look after their interests. He also managed to get me planning permission for a garage and tickets for all-Ireland Gaelic hurling and football finals,

as well as trips to conferences in America and France, petrol vouchers, free cinema tickets, the 'best seats in the house' for myself and Noreen at a Danny Kaye concert in the Hilarity Theatre, and a discount on electricity and phone bills. It was a short but golden period.

CHAPTER 7

Return to Buttery Mountain

In early 1960 a family crisis occurred involving our son Lorcan. He was at that time twenty-four years old, and a student of Irish at University College Dublin. He was a very nice young man, and shared the common glue that cemented the solidity of our family together: the three 's's – strong religious faith, super-nationalism and superb love of the Irish language. I can't say I knew him that well, as that kind of thing was mostly left to Noreen, but from what I saw he seemed to be a normal sort of young fellow. But one day, as Sorcha, Noreen and myself were having our tea, he came to the table grim-faced. He was unable to eat any of the food, and his mother eventually asked if there was anything wrong. 'Mammy and Daddy,' he said eventually, 'I've got a young girl into trouble.' It was literally an absolute bombshell. Immediately I sent Sorcha to her room and tried to bring some kind of order to the situation. Noreen broke down in hysterics and asked for a priest to be called. Father Gerry Dawson had died of an alcohol-related disorder some years before, and I called our new PP, Father Joe Collins. When I reached the parochial house by phone, he was on his way out to a motor-vehicle accident where there had been two fatalities, but he immediately agreed that our need was greater, and he promised that he would arrive as soon as he could. By this time the Guards were on the scene and several neighbours had gathered outside our front gate to see what all the fuss was about. I knew that most of them had guessed what had happened. An awful busybody called Maisie Sheehan who lived about four doors away was all questions: 'Is it the young fella that's in trouble? It's not Sorcha, is it? That fella of yours is in UCD. Did he get one of the girls there into trouble?' I had to tell her to go away in no uncertain terms. Normally the police would arrest the young fellow in this situation, but luckily their man on the scene, Garda Tom Storan, was an old friend of mine, and I promised that I would find out the name of the girl involved and pass it on to him as soon as I could. He agreed with me that as Lorcan was a regular mass-goer, it was probably the lassie that was mostly to blame, and, for the time being anyway, the young man could remain under my custody.

I was mad with panic and despair, but I knew I had to deal with the situation in a firm and disciplined manner. I remembered St Peter's words to the Ephesians to the effect that – I'm paraphrasing here – 'you're in trouble now, lads, but you're just going to have to get your heads down and get on with it'. A reporter who turned up from the *Evening Press* was dealt with by Gloinn, who had cancelled a trip abroad to be on hand for the crisis, a fact for which I will be eternally grateful forever. By this time many of Noreen's relations had started to arrive from Kildare, and accommodation and lodgings had to be arranged. Maire was on hand to deal with this, which she did under Gloinn's close supervision. (Left to her own devices she probably would have booked them into the Shelbourne or the Gresham, thus lumbering me with sky-high bills.)

By this time Lorcan had agreed to be voluntarily tied to his bed, and was answering questions from Doctor Sweetman. As his name suggests, he was a doctor, and it was the only time I ever had dealings with him outside Noreen's numerous crippling illnesses. I was on hand to assist Sweetman in his questioning. Although the GP, like everyone else, must have been under immense strain, he remained very calm and professional while he asked Lorcan the crucial questions: Who led who on? Did he know what his body was doing or was it acting under its own initiative? Had he read about this type of thing in books? (At this point I began to regret the fact that I no longer worked on the Censorship Board, as I certainly would never let anything like that into the country.) Lorcan, however, said that his body seemed to more or less 'take off' under its own steam and that he really didn't know what was going on. Apparently the incident had taken place in a hay barn in Lusk. At this point Father Joe Collins turned up roaring drunk and shouting his head off. It was all a bit much in the circumstances, and I asked him, without of course making any suggestion that he had been drinking, to go home and come back a little later after he'd had a lie down. I never found out how he had managed to get so hopelessly drunk in the twenty or twenty-five minutes since my phone call.

Lorcan, meanwhile, had confessed the name of the girl – Imelda Dunne, who later became a researcher on the BBC's *Newsnight* programme – and as I suspected, it was the young lady who was entirely to blame for the situation. She had suggested that they go into the hay barn while on a day trip with some of Lorcan's pals from UCD. Lorcan said that he didn't want to go into the barn, and only went in the end because he was afraid of his friends laughing at him. One thing led to another inside, and before long the Dunne girl had a 'calf in the paddock'. I managed to contact her father, who naturally went 'apeshit' on hearing the awful news. It was mutually decided that his daughter be packed off to England for the duration of the pregnancy and that the child be put in an orphanage run by nuns in Kent. Considering the dreadful circumstances, everything worked out well enough in the end, even though we were very ashamed that our first grandchild was a bastard. (Although, as Gloinn reminded me, since Noreen and I had adopted Lorcan from an orphanage, in all likelihood he was a bastard as well.)

Thankfully, the episode put Lorcan off sex for life, and he remains a happy celibate to this day in his little home in St John of God's.

Looking back on the affair, I am reminded of how much a catastrophe an unwanted pregnancy was in those days compared to now, and of all the fuss and bother it caused. A bastard born out of wedlock today is as common a sight as full-frontal nudity, and hardly anyone remarks on the fact. I think it's a dirty shame that the stigma attached to bastards is gone and that they're treated more or less the same as everyone else.

Dickie Carr, a friend of mine who worked in the Irish Hospitals Sweepstakes, once confessed to me that despite the fact that he had three daughters, he still wasn't quite sure how they had 'come about'. He said that he didn't really know anything about the facts of life when he married his wife, Margaret, and that he'd mostly relied on instinct. He told me that he'd let his body 'get on with it' when they were in bed, although he was often very afraid of the things it was getting up to. Margaret, of course, was equally petrified, but at least she knew that she didn't have to do anything. Happily, he must have done something right in the end, as their three girls all became nuns!

A very funny incident happened when I went on holiday once with Dickie and Margaret to the Isle of Man. (Noreen was 'dying' in hospital at the time, but subsequently made a miraculous recovery.) Dickie and myself went swimming, and as we were out in the sea, a little dog climbed into Dickie's underpants which he had left on the beach with his other clothes. When Dickie stepped out of the water and hitched his pants up, the wayward pooch found himself pressed into the Irish Hospitals Sweepstakes man's groin. Somehow, he got his teeth into a very tender part of Dickie's anatomy, and wouldn't let go for all the tea in China. The only solution, a lifeguard on the scene insisted, was to shoot the little dog. I still remember the scene; Dickie with the trousers around his ankles, the little terrier clinging on for dear life to his namesake, and the lifeguard aiming the shotgun at the dog's head. You can imagine the agitated state Dickie was in at this stage, as anything less than 100 per cent accuracy would result in carnage not seen since the atom bomb in Hiroshima. Happily, the canine was successfully dispatched, and the Man from the Irish Hospitals Sweepstakes survived intact. The whole affair amused me for weeks. It was a genuinely hilarious incident, the like of which rarely happens nowadays.

The early sixties was the era of the Second Vatican Council. Gloinn, Larry and myself were very interested in events in Rome, as the decisions made would shape the direction of Catholicism for the rest of time. We prayed that all the priests and bishops in Rome would 'get it right'; and not respond to liberal rumblings emanating from 'trendies' within the Hierarchy. I have to say, overall we were disappointed with some of the new ideas which emerged from the council. The subsequent decline of the Latin mass was a deep blow to me personally, while Gloinn described it simply as 'a pain in the *cajones*'. I know Larry was particularly badly hit by the change and went into a deep depression. 'It's not as if it's going to make the mass any more clear to people,' he said to me, exasperated. It seemed that even the Church was changing to suit modern thinking.

A disappointing trend at the time coincided with the increasing amount of cars appearing in Ireland. This made it easier for people in the countryside to seek out short masses in another parish if their own priest was inclined to 'go on a bit' during a service. Thanks to this greater mobility, people would often travel up to fifteen or twenty miles if they knew of a priest who could 'bring in' a mass under half an hour. (By the early 1970s a mass of twenty, or even fifteen, minutes was not unusual.) You can imagine how much this saddened Larry in particular, who loved long masses and would buck the trend by deliberately seeking out mavericks who specialized in marathons. He used often to travel down to Kilcullen in Kildare where Father Denis Boylan did a spectacular three-hour long mass including a legendary meandering sermon which famously veered on and off the point like a racing car driven by a monkey with Alzheimer's disease. Often Larry would be the only member of the congregation, as everyone else had legged it off to a shorter service in a neighbouring parish given by 'quick mass merchants' such as Father Oscar McDevitt in Kiltibbert, who famously could do two masses in ten minutes.

As a result of an article I wrote in *The Cork Examiner* about the changes being brought about by Vatican II, I was asked by the editor of *The Kilkenny Sentinel* to become their sex correspondent. Sex, thanks in no small part to the arrival of *The Late Late Show* on television in 1962, was making inroads into Irish life, often causing confusion, despondency and fear as it had done in other corners of the world where it had reared its ugly head. Again, the words of Michael Judge came into my mind when I embarked on my first column, and I was inspired to call it 'The Hornets' Nest'. I would never propose that mankind can do without sex altogether (otherwise you wouldn't be reading this!), but I think it can be compared to a caged lion tied up in a corner wearing a pair of boxing gloves with razor blades sticking out of them and the lion's probably got a headache at the same time. Even enthusiastic proponents of sex, including those who would describe it as 'a work of art', would have to agree that it is at best a humiliating and at worst an utterly degrading experience. In my column I would chart its rise in Ireland over the following decades through the 'Bishop in a Nightie' incident right up until the revelations of the children allegedly born to Bishop Eamon Casey, Father Michael Cleary, etc., and the trial of my good friend Father Barry Hourican for arms and sex offences.

One man who, as we discovered some years after his death, absolutely loved sex was President John 'JFK' Kennedy, who came to visit Ireland in 1963. It was an absolutely huge moment in the history of the country, and would not be surpassed until the visit of the Holy Father, Pope John Paul II, in 1979, an event organized to a great degree by myself and Gloinn. Of course, at the time we didn't know that Kennedy was 'riding all around him', and we welcomed him into our island home like the returning emigrant he was. I saw him pass down O'Connell Street in a cavalcade – I remember thinking at the time how similar it would be to that fateful one in Dallas a few months later* – and also at his cousin's house in Wexford, where he attended an impromptu, well-rehearsed tea party. As he good-naturedly knocked back the tea and sandwiches and indulged in simple-minded small talk with his ignorant relatives and local hangers-on on that summer's day in the South East, it is strange to realize now that he was probably thinking about riding Judith Exner. In fact, how could he not have been, when the alternative was to try to concentrate on a dreary conversation with Councillor Jim Arselick about his cousin from Arklow in the police force in Boston? It is likely, though unprovable, that President Kennedy had an erection the entire time he was in Ireland, even when he was at events that would have been unlikely to 'turn him on', such as the laying of a wreath in commemoration of the 1916 martyrs at Arbour Hill. Even while listening to a mind-numbingly dull address by the Mayor of Galway, he probably managed to 'keep it up' by fantasizing about being in bed with Marilyn Monroe. But we were unaware of this at the time. He was, as far as we knew, a dutiful Catholic who, through sheer luck, had found himself President of the United States of America.

The Capuchin Fathers subsequently produced a lovely little colour film of his visit. On viewing it again, one is aware of how much the country has changed during the intervening years. Men still wore hats, and priests still comprised a large section (perhaps 25–30 per cent?) of

* President Kennedy was shot and wounded in Dallas in November 1963.

the population. There were few women. They would come later, when the winds of change of the 1960s blew all before them.

Due to the increasing amount of spacecraft being launched into the atmosphere, this was a time when Irish weather began to get very bad. As a result, 'Weather Forecasters' were seen for the first time on RTE television. In my opinion, this was yet another of the many negative and damaging developments in Irish life this century. The average 'Weatherman' or (increasingly) 'Weathergirl' seems inordinately proud of their ability to predict the future, without, of course, taking responsibility for some of the more unpleasant meteorological phenomena such as rain, icy roads and mist or fog. Power without accountability; a depressingly familiar feature of modern Irish life. Anyone who, like me, has been forced to shovel their way out of a snowdrift for almost a week, has good reason to curse their good-humoured dishonesty. Answerable to no one, these weather 'experts' pride themselves on being cleverer than the rest of us, yet when I tried to instigate a civil action against one of these gentlemen a few years ago after a wildly misleading prediction of 'sunny spells' – I developed frostbite while sunbathing as a result – he claimed that weather forecasting involved 'a high risk of inaccuracy'. My dowdy Auntie Maud claimed that she could predict rain by counting the ladders in her stockings, which also no doubt contained a 'high risk of inaccuracy'. The difference is she isn't on television every night of the week being paid millions of pounds by the taxpayer.

Things continued to go wrong with Noreen in the new decade. If she had been an old car, I would have had no option but to bring her down to the quarry and tip her into it. Sadly, however, she wasn't an old car but my wife, and I had no option but to soldier on as best as I could. Something went haywire with her ovaries – God knows why; they'd never been exactly overworked – in the summer of 1964, and Larry suggested that a trip to Lourdes might be in order. This I thought was an excellent idea, and together with Gloinn, who was making his eighty-fifth visit, Maire, who had slimmed down to fourteen stone especially for the occasion, and Father Joe Collins, we set off for France.

Lourdes was an intoxicating place. I remember thinking that it was probably what Las Vegas would have been like if casinos and nightclubs had been replaced by Catholicism. I was mesmerized by the vast amount of candles and wheelchairs and the general sense of unwellbeing. It seemed strange to be in a place that was so Catholic and yet non-Irish.

We went for a beautiful afternoon tea in an outdoor café on the day we arrived, and I remember Noreen being absolutely fascinated by some straws that were on the table in a glass. She had never seen straws before and stared at them for at least half an hour. However, she was too frightened to 'try them out' and since she only drank tea, she said that she would only be wasting them anyway.

An unfortunate incident occurred as I was pushing Noreen's wheelchair down a hill on the day after our arrival. I foolishly let go for a split second, and Noreen flew off at top speed. Her rapid descent was thankfully blocked by a group of semi-dead pensioners from Scotland on their way back from confession. There was an awful crunching sound as she hit them at what must have been upwards of forty miles an hour. The bones of the oldsters must have been as brittle as a dry leaf in the Sahara desert, but miraculously (we were in the right place for that type of thing!) no one was badly injured, except for one old lady who died. As people were dropping like flies in Lourdes every minute of the day (Gloinn likened the high pilgrim turnover to the first day of the Battle of the Somme), this particular demise was hardly noticed.

I have often wondered why I let go of Noreen's wheelchair in such a cavalier fashion. I remember thinking at the time, 'I'll just let go now and see what happens.' Was it some subconscious desire to rid myself of Noreen and all her problems? I shall probably never know.

During the third or fourth day of our visit, Larry returned to our hotel in a highly excited state. He swore that he had seen 'a man who had grown a leg'. His story was that he had been down in the grotto where he had seen a one-legged man sitting on a wall some distance away. Larry waved to him and the old timer returned his greeting with a doff of his cap. A few minutes later, Larry saw the same man in the water, and lo and behold, didn't he now have two legs! There was no doubt about it – it was an absolute miracle and wasn't Larry the lucky man to have seen it. Later on, Gloinn wondered if Larry had finally gone 'off his rocker', as he was sure that our old friend must have imagined the whole thing. Larry often wanted to believe that many things that had happened to him were miracles. If he got the wrong change in a shop, he would often claim that it was a miracle, especially if he had received too much money rather than too little. 'Look at this Eoin,' he would say. 'I got one and six there when I should have got only one and five. God is looking after me all right. Sure isn't it a miracle.' Most of the time I didn't have the heart to disagree with him, and perhaps – who knows – maybe once or twice he may have even been right.

As if things weren't bad enough, Noreen went blind in the harsh winter of 1964 after being hit on the head by a snowball with a rock in it. Thankfully, it was only a temporary condition, but it still caused me lots of inconvenience. For a while, we employed a housekeeper, Mrs Shortley, who, I must admit, I had a lot of trouble with. She was a very rude woman in her late fifties, and was usually in the foulest of foul moods. Predictably, the causes of her irritability were 'women's troubles'. (Later I found out that she had a dilapidated womb.) She lived with us for the period of her employment, and used to carry on with an old sailor called Sidney that she had met in a pub. He was a real 'rogue' and was almost as unpleasant as she was. I heard afterwards from Garda Storan that before he had met Mrs Shortley he had chased dogs into corners in pubs where he would 'try things on with them', usually cheered on by some of his old seafaring chums who would give him a few shillings for entertaining them. Most unpleasant stuff, and I was never pleased to see him when he would come a-calling on Mrs Shortley. One time I heard them kissing in her room and had little choice but to investigate the matter further. I crawled to her door and peered through the keyhole, being careful to make as little noise as possible. Of course, I hadn't bargained for the fact that both herself and Sidney would be naked. (Mrs Shortley, to be absolutely accurate, was technically semi-naked, as she wore a rather dirty bra that was far too small for her.) It was a grim spectacle indeed, but I thought I could turn the incident to my advantage by using it to put Sorcha and Lorcan off sex. I woke them from their beds and ushered them downstairs so that they could see what a nasty business stark-naked physical interaction is. 'Take a good look at that, Lorcan and Sorcha,' I said, pointing to the keyhole. 'Take a good long hard look. And then tell me, would you like to picture yourself in that situation?' They each took a turn at peeking through the aperture, then shook their heads in a dazed state before returning upstairs to their beds. It is fair to say they were both very badly shaken. Next day, they told me that they both had terrible nightmares. Two weeks later Lorcan had the first of several nervous breakdowns which would eventually lead to his long-term incarceration.

While Lorcan gradually withdrew from the real world, Sorcha was becoming a very different basket of eggs. By the mid-1960s she had graduated from UCD with an arts degree and had moved to a flat in Rathmines. This was the time of 'the pill' and 'free love', and soon, to my deep horror, Sorcha was becoming a propagandist for these alien ideas. I wondered aloud to Noreen whether it was too late to send her back to the orphanage, but after going through the adoption papers, we realized that it wasn't a realistic option to send a woman in her mid-twenties back to the Bastard Shop. One day in the kitchen at home, the same happy little room where she had drunk milk and munched tomato sandwiches during her childhood years, Sorcha admitted to me that she had given up going to mass and had gone to bed with her boyfriend Thomas. In fact, she had gone to bed with Thomas *instead* of going to mass! We subsequently had a fierce shouting match during which Noreen was accidentally shot in the face (I forget the exact details of how this happened), but inevitably another spell in hospital for Mammy ensued. This, of course, occurred at another extremely inconvenient time for me: the first amalgamated euthanasia/abortion conference, which, chaired by Father Dick Bugnanany, who had made a fool of Gay Byrne on *The Late Late Show* the previous week, promised to be a bundle of laughs. (I went anyway, leaving Noreen to find her own way to Casualty.) To think that *both* of my unmarried children had had sex while their parents remained virgins enraged me to the point where I considered, for the first and only time in my life, going down to the pub with Gloinn and drowning my sorrows in the whiskey bottle. I was soon on the phone to various Catholic organizations, looking for some kind of parental 'troubleshooting' help, but apparently there was a Rolling Stones concert in Dublin the same week and they had their hands full.

Over the following years, Sorcha's antics would continue to enrage me. Influenced by liberals such as Peg
'Five Bellies' McCandless and 'Burn your Bra' brigaders
like Mary Kenny, she fell victim to the full horrors
of sixties liberalism, once even accusing me of a pro-
American stance over Vietnam, whereas, of course, I
didn't give a damn one way or the other. Gloinn had
'filled me in' on this one: 'They might be Communists,
all right, Eoin, but sure they're so far away they might as
well be on the moon!'* I remember thinking at the time
that a lot of the 'feminesbians' that Sorcha hung out
with were singularly unattractive, or indeed, downright
ugly, girls, and I have noticed that many of them have
failed to marry over the years. But then again, what man
would wish to marry a woman who would feed him on
a diet of pitta bread and apple juice? Thankfully, Sorcha
(like the aforementioned Miss Kenny) has mellowed
over the years, and now realizes that everything she believed in in the 1960s was horseshit. She is now happily
married to an Irish (the language, not the nationality! –
although he's that as well) lecturer in Cork, and has
given me two delightful grandchildren, Aislaunacheen
and Duirbheuiannuineonn.

**A very, very funny incident happened to me a few years
ago when I was at an All-Ireland Club-Hurling semi-final
match in Thurles with four-year-old Aislaunacheen. During**

* He later changed his mind after reading a pamphlet on Communist China by Father Ned Rush, who had spent some time in
Shanghai where he had been tortured by the authorities.

the half-time interval she said that she really needed to use the toilet and would I take her to the Ladies. I have to say I wasn't entirely sure what to do in such unprecedented circumstances, and I remember thinking 'this is one part of being a grandfather I can do without!' Finally, after a bit of a walk, we arrived at the female lavatory, and I decided to wait and ask a woman to take little Aislaunacheen in with her. Unfortunately though, there were precious few women present at what I remember being a particularly crunching and brutal display of hurling, and I found my situation becoming more and more daunting. However, I thought my worries were over when I saw a kindly looking nun approach. 'Excuse me, Sister,' I said. 'Would you mind taking this little girl with you into the Gents?' The nun looked at me in some puzzlement for a moment or two and I began to wonder if I'd said something wrong. After a second, of course, I realized that through sheer force of habit I'd said 'Gents' instead of 'Ladies'. I was mortified! However, I managed to hide my embarrassment and immediately apologized for my error. The nun was absolutely fine about it, and happily agreed to take my little grandchild in for a 'wee'. I think any funny story is immediately improved if there's a nun involved, and this hilarious incident, I think, is a perfect example! When I told Gloinn afterwards he nearly split his sides with the laughter, and it is an episode that I am sure he will never let me forget!

CHAPTER 8

Piper at the Gates of Drumcroom

My 'Hornets' Nest' column had been running for several years in *The Kilkenny Sentinel* when I got a call from the editor asking me to take part in a *Late Late Show* debate on sex. The column had been getting quite a reaction not just locally, but nationwide, after some of the more noteworthy passages had been reprinted in the national press. *The Late Late Show* was to feature me and Sister Anulta McSpain, representing the Church, a young pro-contraceptive married couple from Dublin and Hugo Mountpatrick, a Protestant landowner typical of the sort who, despite his vast inheritance acquired through the suffering of the local Catholic population over centuries, constantly moans about how much it costs to maintain his fifty-bedroomed country pile. Gay Byrne, as ever, was the host. Gloinn accompanied me on my trip out to the RTE Studios to lend me support, though I secretly suspected that he was a tiny bit envious that I, rather than him, had been chosen to represent the moral majority. As we left the car park, we spotted Terry Wogan, at that time still working in RTE, leaving the building. Gloinn didn't want to see him, as he had got into a rather undignified scuffle with the light entertainer at Dublin airport a few weeks before, so he hid in the bushes until Wogan had passed.

I was a bit worried that I would become nervous under the 'bright lights' of Studio 1, but as the show progressed I soon forgot everything in the white heat of debate. Emotions were certainly running high on the evening, and as events unfolded – eventually leading to the intervention of the Gardai – it is fair to say that Gay Byrne had his work well and truly cut out to keep the situation from careering out of control. Despite our obvious differences, relations between the panellists were cordial enough until our Protestant friend made a remark which I took to be a slight on Archbishop McQuaid. (I recall that he described the Archbishop as a 'mud lark' or something similar.) To give a flavour of the debate, I shall reprint the relevant part of my sub-sequent play in Irish, *A La Na Gan Anois An Late Late Show* (*It All Started on The Late Late Show*) which deals with events that night and the subsequent trial. (Unfortunately, when I later tried to get a tape of the show from RTE, they informed me that the programme had been 'wiped'.)

Gay Byrne: (*Very professional*) Mr Mountpatrick, you've had dealings with Archbishop McQuaid in the past. I believe he intervened to stop you getting planning permission for a rabbit hutch on your estate at Multymore.

Mountpatrick: (*Arrogant tone*) Yes, indeed. I thought it was an unnecessary intervention. To my mind, the Archbishop is little more than a mud lark.

O'Ceallaigh: (*Heroic, confident*) I will not have the Archbishop of Dublin described in such a way on national television.

We hear faint murmuring from cowed pro-contraceptive married couple.

Mountpatrick: If I may be allowed to quote Yeats here . . .

O'Ceallaigh: There'll be no quoting of Yeats in this place. The Irish people have spoken, and their faith is in the Bishops and the fallen heroes of 1916.

Voice from audience: (*Gloinn McTire*) He has you on the run, Mountpatrick! You pigeon fancying* Freemason!
Muted clapping in crowd.

O'Ceallaigh: They should have burnt you out in '22!
Muted clapping in crowd builds to crescendo.

Gay Byrne: (*Trying to change the subject by introducing popular singing group, The Bachelors*) Now, we have some old friends of ours back tonight . . .
Snoring from Sister Anulta, still asleep since ad break.

Voice from audience: (*McTire again*) Buck lepers one and all!

O'Ceallaigh: Come outside and settle this now, Mountpatrick!
Mountpatrick rises from his chair and jumps over desk to attack O'Ceallaigh. McTire leaps into fray from audience. Chaos ensues. The Bachelors wait unsurely in the wings as Gay Byrne consults with his producer. Fistfights break out and the Gardai arrive on scene.

Yes, it was all very heady stuff, and while I may have overdramatized, or indeed, invented, certain small details, I think the play (which unfortunately remains

---

* Mountpatrick was one of Ireland's most noted pigeon breeders.

unproduced) gives an accurate portrayal of the proceedings. At the resulting trial, I was acquitted of libel, but Gloinn was unfortunately convicted on three charges of assault on Mountpatrick and the pro-contraceptive couple. I was never again invited to appear on *The Late Late Show*, though, like most of the population, I tuned in regularly over the years to watch a programme which I believe has never been bettered in the field of quality family entertainment.

Myself and Gloinn's appearance on the programme, followed by the publicity generated by the trial, got us both noticed by the media and the public at large, though, of course, within Catholic circles, we had been well known for quite some time.

A peculiar by-product of becoming a bit of a celebrity was that I was asked by RTE to become the face on their television test card; a type of Irish version of the girl beside the blackboard on the BBC. This test card was 'on the telly' when there weren't any programmes on, so that the viewer would know that his television wasn't broken. Most people, not surprisingly, thought that my face *was* some kind of programme, and many elderly ladies living alone, especially, would watch 'me' for hours. A friend of mine said to me recently that he wished my test card face was still on, as it would be a lot better than most of the programmes that are transmitted today! I have to say, I agreed with him wholeheartedly! Another old lady I met a year or so ago said to me that she didn't know how I kept still for so long. I had to explain to her that they had used

a photograph and that it wasn't a 'live-action' programme of me sitting on a chair! She turned a very bright shade of scarlet when I pointed out her error. I have noticed that old ladies have a habit of getting things wrong, and their confusion can often be very amusing.

In 1970, my father died after swallowing a razor blade hidden in a bag of chips. I had not been close to him for some time, though of course we met at family occasions, such as Sorcha's marriage, a matter of weeks before his death. The Black and Tan incident of fifty years before still rankled with me, and had been the major incentive for my initiative to instigate a cutback in the old-age pension in the late 1950s when I was working at the Department of Welfare. There was no particular need for a cutback in this particular area, but I managed to persuade the minister at the time that it would be a great idea. Of course, the real reason was that I knew it would cause my father tremendous hardship. Sorcha has said to me more than once that I have an unusual ability to hold a grudge, and on this occasion she was certainly right! The old man ended up out on the streets, having to fend for himself by begging and drawing useless child-like reproductions of masterpieces by Rembrandt on the wet pavement with chalk for the amusement of passing tourists. Of course, my mother suffered as well, but unfortunately there are always 'civilian casualties' in situations like these, and I was helpless to come to her aid. After I felt my father had been taught enough of a lesson, I persuaded the minister that I had made a bookkeeping error and, in fact, there was no reason to cut the old-age pension at all. He immediately increased it again, and before long my parents were able to move back indoors. My father later found out through an article in *The RTE Guide* that it was me who was the cause of his misfortune, and this increased the ill-feeling between us even further.

After my father's death, my mother moved to a nursing home in Lucan. She would have been around the eighty mark at this point, but was still in quite good health. Her hair had remained jet black until she was well into her seventies, but she'd seen a rock act called, I think, The Crazy World of Arthur Brown, on *Top of the Pops*, while passing by the window of a TV/Electrical shop in O'Connell Street, and this had given her a tremendous shock, causing her locks to immediately turn a blinding white. There was no way that a woman of her background could withstand something like that, and I don't think she ever really recovered from it. Recently, on a nostalgia-based pop music programme on Channel 4 – though God knows how anyone could be nostalgic about stuff like that – I saw this *Top of the Pops* performance by Arthur Brown, and it is really quite, quite mad. Here is a fella, who basically looks like the Devil, jumping around like a lunatic with his hair on fire. What the hell would be going through his head, I wondered, as I watched it. And, of course, I'm told that some of the pop acts around now* are even worse!

* Westlife and B*Witched.

My mother died in 1973 after a lacklustre and half-hearted battle against illness. She had been very sick for about six months, and I managed to persuade her that a trip to Lourdes would be a great boost for her. The doctors warned me that she would be too weak to travel, and in all likelihood would not survive the journey, but I wouldn't listen to a word they said, as in my experience doctors are usually wrong about everything. However, in this case, they were right, and she died on the runway at Lourdes airport.

The funeral was a simple (and, at my insistence, an inexpensive) affair, and she was buried beside Daddy in Glasnevin cemetery. The beautiful funeral mass was said by a very drunk Father Joe Collins, who himself died at the small reception held afterwards in the Glenworth Hotel in Santry. I knew that my mother would not have wanted the wake/reception to turn into a drunken brawl as often happens on these occasions, so I had limited the alcohol on offer to two bottles of Guinness. By the time Father Collins arrived, Gloinn had already downed these – rather needlessly, I thought, as he had brought his own supply – and the cleric went into the foulest of foul moods. He ended up finding drink somewhere, and was discovered early the next morning, dead in a jumbo bin outside the hotel. As is all too common in clerical deaths, alcohol poisoning was the cause of his demise, and a few days later I found myself at his funeral, conducted by Father Dinny Cauldwell, who was also, sadly, obviously very drunk. Gloinn told me once that the 'record' for priests saying mass at a funeral and then dying of alcohol poisoning at the reception afterwards is four, e.g., Priest A* says mass at a funeral, then dies at reception. Priest B says mass at Priest A's funeral, then dies at reception. Priest C says mass at Priest B's funeral, then dies at reception. Priest D says mass at Priest C's funeral, then dies at reception. The 'domino' effect here is very noticeable, and I think it's something that, as a trend, is peculiar to the Irish clergy. No doubt some newspaper will at some future date conduct an 'investigation' into the subject in a further attempt to humiliate the Hierarchy.

My life has never been predictable, but early in 1971 I got what still remains the biggest shock of my life. Noreen, through some absolutely freak accident, had become pregnant. The chances of a 56-year-old woman getting pregnant are slim enough, but how on God's earth could a 56-year-old woman get pregnant without having sex? Since I obviously hadn't gone anywhere near her, the only reason I could think of was that she had come into contact with semen somewhere, perhaps in a factory or a shed, and that it had soaked through her skin and done the dirty on her that way. I honestly couldn't work out what else could have happened. Doctor Sweetman was as puzzled as I was, while Noreen was in a terrible state. Then, just as mysteriously as it had appeared, her pregnancy went away again. I have never found a satisfactory explanation for the crazy event, and I have come to accept it as a sign from God, either

---

* Names available from publisher on request.

thanking us for being good Catholics, or punishing us for doing something bad (the incident with my father springs to mind). Whatever it was – Sweetman came to believe it had something to do with Noreen's bizarre hormone imbalances – it was an episode that shook us badly, not only at the time, but also later, when we saw the film *Rosemary's Baby* on television. It would have just been like Noreen to complicate my life further by giving birth to the Antichrist.

A very welcome distraction from my troubles at that time was found in another collaboration with Gloinn. This was a non-religious activity that we did just for a 'bit of fun', and we both enjoyed it immensely.

Gloinn during this period was living in Naas with Maire, where he was working on his biography of Sister Ursula Cascarino, an unheralded heroine of the Great Famine of the 1840s who encouraged the starving to die rather than accept Protestant soup (potential converts were also promised fancy cakes). There was a very entertaining and inoffensive programme on RTE at the time called *Tops of the Team*, where local amateur drama/ musical groups from around the country would compete with each other for the prestigious *Tops of the Team* trophy and a cheque for five pounds. Gloinn suggested that I get together with him and his local group in Naas and work on writing a suitable show to put on in front of the RTE cameras. We decided that it would be a great idea to mount a show based on Larry, whose life had inspired us so much over the years. An 'all-singing, all-dancing' tribute to his tremendous work for the poor would not just entertain, but also hopefully show the merits of a life so inspired by, and dedicated to, God. We called the show, quite simply, *Larry*. Our little group comprised Gloinn, myself, Maire and three other locals: two men and three girls. Needless to say, the girls didn't have to be encouraged to take part in the dance numbers (choreographed by Gloinn, who up until that time had no interest in dancing at all!). Meanwhile, I had assumed the 'George Gershwin' role, and was busily writing all the words and lyrics to the songs. There was an early setback when Maire, as part of the chorus, unwisely jumped high into the air (against Gloinn's expressed instructions) and on her return journey crash-landed right through the floor of the stage, causing several hundred pounds' worth of damage. Bizarrely, the previous week, she had fallen from the window of their bedroom and crashed through their greenhouse. Gloinn was quite rightly furious with her for demolishing the stage, but also relieved that her broken legs and arms would force her out of the show. She had rather pestered him to let her be involved, but we both knew that she would lose us marks just by the look of her alone. She was replaced by Mrs Dunning, the wife of the local chemist, who, by a stroke of luck, had a beautiful tenor voice.

The show consisted of three acts (the classic musical 'structure'): Larry's life growing up in the slums of Dublin, his time working in Dublin Corporation, and his later years helping the city's poor. After we had come up with this initial 'scene breakdown', Gloinn and I were

sure that we were destined to put on a cracking entertainment every bit as good as *The Sound of Music* or *The
King and I*. We even started work on a screenplay which
we intended sending to Hollywood. I thought Yul Bryn-
ner would make a perfect Larry for the screen version,
and we even wrote ourselves small roles. (When I told
Noreen about this, she said, 'Who's going to play you
two? Laurel and Hardy I suppose!' This was a very funny
remark; one of only two she made in almost fifty years
of marriage.) I wrote seventeen songs for the show, in
hindsight maybe too many for a ten-minute performance, but there were some gems amongst them, including 'Larry's Song', 'God Help the Poor' and 'Dublin
Corporation Blues'. Considering I haven't got a tune in
my head, and had never written a song before in my life,
I think I did superbly well. I admit that it may not have
been Rodgers and Hart, but it wasn't Rodgers and
O'Finnegan (a team of very bad songwriters from Letter-
kenny) either. If anything let us down on the night, it
was Gloinn's somewhat leaden choreography coupled
with the fact that we got what in showbusiness terms is
called 'the wrong audience'. Also, we lost all the cos-
tumes in a fire before the show, and, at the last minute,
Gerry Swords, playing the major role of trade-union
leader Jim Larkin, decided he didn't want to do it. Plus,
we were up against some stiff competition: a musical
about Malcolm X from Navan (featuring, as I later found
out, a young Pierce Brosnan) and a very daring Japanese
Noh theatre version of *The Birds* from Strabane.

We invited Larry to the dress rehearsal on the afternoon of the show and, to be honest, he *hated* it. I was disappointed by his reaction, but Gloinn and I were sure that it was only because seeing oneself portrayed on stage must be rather unsettling for the individual concerned. Apparently Cole Porter went through a similar experience when he sat rather uncomfortably through the premiere of *Night and Day*. I also found out afterwards that Larry had been cycling around Fairview that morning, and had stopped to investigate a magazine sticking out of a ditch. It turned out to be a pornographic magazine, and this put him in very bad form for the rest of the day. Despite the indifferent audience, the fact that we got no marks, and RTE's decision not to actually transmit the show on television because it was 'unbroadcastable', it was still a worthwhile experience and it at least stopped me thinking about Noreen's freak pregnancy.

After our brief career in 'the business we call *show*', Gloinn and I started up another Catholic magazine entitled *Catholicism Today*. An ambitious plan had been forming in my head for a while at this stage, and we decided to use the magazine to promote it.

This was the mid-1970s, a time when the Irish people were very much in need of spiritual renewal. Dana had won the Eurovision Song Contest a few years before with a song that she seemed to be more or less making up as she went along, but since that glorious night, there had been little to write home about. (I call it a Eurovision Song Contest, but it was little more than a selection of entrants singing songs from their native country, and then being awarded marks by a panel of judges). Young people were walking around with long hair and flared trousers, the politicians didn't seem to give a damn about anything, and Northern Ireland was going up in flames around us, a victim of the Unionists' inability to combat the fetid stagnation of what my friend, the nationalist poet Cal Og O'Glume, has called 'a thimble reckoning, a putrid boil on the bullstrode of philostry. A gnat-arsed type of thing; a virus; a fountain of rectitude in the tepid air of loss.' The failure of the Sunningdale initiative of 1973 seemed to illustrate once more the singular myth of – to quote O'Glume again – 'bug-eyed sentimentalism. A cross; a conglomerate [sic]; a vestibule; an argument leaning on a gate. The swans are dead, A Gnaiste. The lion is in his box.'

Whilst watching an unremarkable episode of *The Rockford Files* at home one grey day in 1975 as Maire lay groaning on the floor in the kitchen after a mishap with an electric whisk (I had already helped her up three times that day, and I wasn't about to do it again), the thought suddenly struck me; why not invite the Pope to visit Ireland? It was a simple but inspired notion that just came to me right out of the blue, from where I do not know (God?). I was on the phone in an instant to Gloinn, who surprised me by being initially sceptical about the idea. At this time, Pope Paul VI was still the Man in Charge, and while nowadays we are well used to the current incumbent whizzing around the globe as if there is no tomorrow (and he may know something we don't about that – maybe there isn't) at that time the pontiff – invariably an Italian lad – did little but wander slowly from room to room around the Vatican testing out the plush carpets in his linen slippers. He would rarely venture outside, except to make occasional visits to Castlegandolfo for the fly-fishing. This was the popular view of the papacy which was firmly lodged in Gloinn's mind, and it took a great effort on my part to change his attitude. By this time, we had lost Archbishop McQuaid, who had gone to the larger diocese in the sky a couple of years previously, so he was unfortunately unavailable to aid our venture. We missed Doctor McQuaid's steadying hand, but wished him 'all the best' in the next world. Of course, since his death there have been the usual rumours circulating,* but really, like the footballer with butterflies in his stomach before he goes out on to the pitch, the time to really start worrying is when there are no allegations!

The new man in charge of the Dublin diocese was a youngster barely out of his fifties, but we got on with him very well and were very confident that we could influence the authorities to put our plan into action. The next day I wrote a lead article in *Catholicism Today* under the headline 'Why not Invite the Pope to Ireland'. I deliberately left out the question mark, so that the sentence would appear rhetorical, and thus firmly plant the idea in people's minds. Needless to say, myself and Gloinn were soon all over the radio, television and newspapers expounding on our initiative, and there was

* Paedophilia and homosexuality.

a real buzz of expectancy in the air. I remember a headline in one of the newspapers which said something to the effect of 'Will the Pope Come to Ireland?' On a radio programme I was asked a question along the lines of 'do you think the Pope will come to Ireland?' Often I was stopped on the street and people would ask me things like 'The Pope, he's up there in the Vatican, isn't he? . . . Do you think he will come to Ireland?'

My reply was always the same: 'I just don't know.' All this talk about whether the Pope would come to Ireland was rendered redundant just two years later when Pope Paul died. 'All right,' I remember saying to Gloinn, '*that* Pope won't be coming to Ireland, but there'll be another one along, and he might come.' Tragically, the reign of Pope John Paul I was to be a short one. He was ruthlessly murdered after he fell foul of the Vatican bank in a scene straight out of *Godfather III*.

Amidst an eerie sensation of déjà vu, I remember saying to Gloinn, 'All right, *that* Pope won't be coming to Ireland, but there'll be another one along, and he might come.' It would be a case of third time lucky.

1975 saw the death of Eamon de Valera. He had been blind and mad for decades, but had still spent most of that time in public office. In his later years, as President, he would meet and greet visiting heads of state, most of the time not having the remotest clue who they were. On shaking hands with Charles de Gaulle, the French President was quizzed on questions about golf, camels, and Dorothy Lamour. Apparently Dev thought he was Bing Crosby.

I saw him for the last time just three months before he died. He had gone to see out his final days with nuns in a nursing home where he was more or less left to his own devices. I was shocked when I saw him. His fingernails were four or five inches long, his hair had grown almost down to his shoulders, and he was dressed in rags. A nun told me he refused to leave his room and answered only to the name of Charlotte. He spent much of his time in the evenings, after a supper of stale biscuits and water, barking like a dog. I had called on him to enquire if he would be willing to sign a blank petition which I had prepared. He asked me why it was blank and I replied that I would fill in the details later. The idea was basically that it would be used after his death to lend his support to ideas he had promoted in his lifetime such as the constitutional bans on divorce and contraception. (A similar scheme in Spain subsequently worked with Franco.) Dev agreed to my proposal and promptly signed. Some time later, after his death, I located the petition so that I could give his support from beyond the grave to the anti-abortion 1983 constitutional amendment. I was disappointed to discover that the piece of paper was useless. Dev, obviously in a state of dementia, had signed his name 'Deputy Dawg'. This was a cartoon character I remember seeing on the television in his room the day I had visited him. It was an error I had not noticed at the time.

His funeral later that year was a solemn affair. Outside the Pro-Cathedral after the service, I talked to an old friend of Dev's, Packie MacConnell, who had fought with the Anti-Treatyites during the civil war. 'This is all very sad, Eoin,' he said to me. 'I hope my funeral is different. I'd like the government to organize something like the carnival in Rio de Janeiro, with singing and dancing and samba bands and everyone out of their heads on Tequila.' After this conversation, I remember thinking two things: that Packie's view of himself and his role in Irish history was perhaps overinflated, and that his plans for his own funeral were quite mad. When he did die, he was buried in a white 'economy' coffin on a wet and windy day in Moate with five people at his graveside. Two of these were only there because he'd owed them money, and this was their last chance to get some of it back from his widow.

Around the beginning of 1979, word filtered through to myself and Gloinn that it was increasingly likely that Pope John Paul (II) would be coming to Ireland. The sheer feeling of joy we felt when we heard the news would be simply impossible to describe. Gloinn did a headstand, then rolled around on the ground in ecstasy for minutes like a Brazilian soccer player celebrating a goal resulting from a 'banana' kick. We were mightily pleased. By sheer determination, we had succeeded in our ambition to bring the Holy Father to the birthplace of Catholicism. The New Man seemed like a great choice. Not just extremely conservative, but a professional goalkeeper to boot! When I read he was Polish, I was confused at first, as I initially took the wrong meaning from the word – 'polish', as in 'Go outside and polish your shoes, Seamus, you're not going to the funeral looking like that.' But, of course, I soon realized that he was

'Polish' only in the sense that he came from Poland. There were other things we liked about him, too. The fact that he was born and grew up in a cold climate meant that, like the Irish, he would not be 'hot-blooded', and therefore more unlikely to have sexual inclinations than an Italian pope, which, of course, would make him less prone to blackmail. (The Italians generally are a very 'sexy' people – not an accusation you could make about the Irish!)

In the months preceding his visit, I wrote several letters to the newspapers proposing that Protestants in the country might wish to spend the duration of his visit with their brethren in Northern Ireland, thus rendering our little state 'Protestant Free', something that I'm sure would have thrilled the Holy Father greatly. This, predictably, met with howls of protests from the dour Prods, who, not content with making the country less Catholic, seemed determined to stay in it at a time when the head of the majority religion was coming on a visit! Apart from the sheer bad manners involved in this action (which I likened at the time to a display of petulance from a ten-year-old when he's told he can't sit in his father's favourite armchair) it seemed the minority was trying to dictate terms to the majority by a provocative display which demonstrated little more than contempt for the proportional representation mandate which had been bestowed on Irish Catholics, not just by the government, but by God as well. Some of the 'bearded intellectuals' then coming into prominence in *The Irish Times* castigated me for daring to speak up for Catholics at the very moment when they (the bearded intellectuals) were trying desperately to loosen the grip of the clergy on the Irish people, through their whingeing columns and frequent television appearances where they would moan about censorship and priests. They were very much the new breed of left wingers who at the time were wasting their energies on hilarious capers such as the preservation of the old Wood Quay Viking part of Dublin. (Vikings? Who gives a damn!) Divorce, conversation and abortion were also 'high on their agenda', and it was clear that the country was about to enter a dark age of liberalism unless the majority were prepared to put up a fight. The arrival of Pope John Paul (II) in the summer of 1979 was a not to be missed opportunity to wave papal flags in the faces of the hairy heathens.

Gloinn and I were determined that the Pope's first impressions of Ireland should be good ones, and we desperately hoped that on his trip from the airport into Dublin he wouldn't see any learner drivers with their L plates stuck on sideways to their back windscreens. Such a display of ignorance – sadly an all too common sight on Irish roads – could easily provoke an anti-Irish remark or joke from a member of the papal entourage, or even from the Holy Father himself. It has always been a source of wonder to me how many Irish motorists stick on their L plates sideways. If they can't master the rather simple art of sticking on an L plate the right way up, then how on God's earth do they expect to pass their driving test? I suspect that this type of one-letter dyslexia is peculiar to the Irish, as I cannot

recall coming across it on any of my travels abroad. There seems to be no rational explanation for it, although it may be in some way linked to post-colonialism.

And so, as if in a dream, he came amongst us. Who will ever forget that wonderful moment when the Man from Rome (via Krakow) knelt down on his knees and kissed the tarmac at Dublin airport? Not anyone who was there, certainly (which, of course, included myself, Noreen, Maire, Larry and Gloinn), nor the billions who watched it live on radio and television. I remember thinking at the time 'the new Pope's gone mad!' but of course it was just his way of saying a 'big hello and thanks very much!' to the people of Ireland who had done so much to keep popes in a job over the years. It is hard to think of a more momentous moment in world history.

The day of the papal mass in Phoenix Park stirred memories of the Eucharistic Congress held at the same venue all those years before. It was where I had first met Larry, and where Gloinn and myself had become aware of the need for vigilance against alien unCatholic forces. How strange that word looks as I write it now; 'un-Catholic' – the small and insignificant 'un' against the overwhelming might and power of the word 'Catholic'. It seems almost crazy to juxtapose the two words together to form another word, even though, technically 'un' isn't a word at all, but merely a part of a word. However, the word (or phrase, or whatever it is) is something that has been heard increasingly in the last thirty years, and is not the strange, unfamiliar thing it once was.

In the park, the Big Pole said a wonderful (and long – Larry loved it!) mass, and who can ever forget the hilarious (though dignified) spectacle of the Pope travelling around in his 'Popemobile' waving insanely at the Irish. Not anyone who was there, certainly (which, of course, included myself, Noreen, Maire, Larry and Gloinn), nor the billions who watched it live on radio and television. I remember thinking at the time 'is that some kind of ice-cream van?' and half expected Larry (who had gone rather senile at this stage) to wander over to the vehicle and ask for a choc ice and a couple of cones!

Shortly after the Phoenix Park event, Pope John Paul (II) spoke to the Young People of Ireland at Galway in another marathon mass that, quite simply, had everything. At the end of the concelebration, he delivered a wonderful, completely off-the-cuff, speech on topics as diverse as the importance of staying a virgin to resisting sex (even) in marriage (great! I winked at Noreen) in a veritable tour de force of Catholic teaching. Who can forget the extraordinary effect that he had on the Young People that day? Not anyone who was there, certainly (which, of course, included myself, Noreen, Maire, Larry and Gloinn), nor the billions who watched it live on radio and television. I remember thinking at the time 'he's not going to be able to top this', but a few days later he 'pulled it out of the hat' again, when he went to Maynooth to talk to priests at the seminary there. Who

can forget the thrilling sight of the seminarians completely losing the run of themselves and bursting out in
a spontaneous version of *You'll Never Walk Alone* when
they were exposed to the greatness of the ex-goalkeeper
and stern anti-Communist? Not anyone who was there,
certainly (which, of course, included myself, Noreen,
Maire, Larry and Gloinn), nor the billions who watched
it live on radio and television. I remember thinking at
the time 'this fella is one of the best popes ever', and it
really was tremendous watching him in action. It was
definitely one of the greatest days that Maynooth has
ever seen.

It was after this event that Gloinn, Larry and I were to
be introduced to the Top Man at a small private audience; something that had been arranged by the then
Cardinal, His Excellence, Tomas Cardinal O'Fiach.
Gloinn said this was something that he felt would crown
a lifetime in Catholicism, and, while obviously absolutely thrilled at the prospect, we were also sick with
nerves. Maire and Noreen had pestered us with requests
to get autographs ('just ask him to put "to Maire"'), but
it was not my intention to lumber the Pontiff with
superfluousness of that kind. The plan was really just to
say 'hello' to him, and then, as Cardinal O'Fiach said (of
course good-humouredly) just 'feck off'. If he wanted to
talk to us about specific work we'd done over the years
or anything similar, then great, but we didn't want to
waste his valuable time. I just hoped Gloinn wouldn't
get into an interminable chat with him about a subject
in which the Holy Father had no interest: something

which had happened when he'd met Hitler and started rabbiting on to him about the government's Irish-language policy.

The great moment was almost upon us when a misfortune befell Gloinn which caused his prospects of a long chinwag with the Pontiff to go up the Swanee. He has suffered for years from a medical condition, though harmless and non life-threatening, which has caused him much discomfort. There may or may not be a proper term for this malady, but he himself has simply called it having a 'wet arse'. It is something which has also affected me on and off over the years, and I know that many others suffer from it, although it seems to afflict Gloinn more than most. Basically it occurs after a visit to the toilet to do a 'number 2'. One cleans the anal cavity to the best of one's ability, but after cleaning, a sensation of 'wetness' returns later, causing discomfort and a desire to, as Gloinn says, 'give the hole a rub'. There is usually no problem if one is near a lavatory with toilet paper, but on this occasion, while we were only seconds away from meeting our spiritual leader, there seemed no hope of relief. Not alone a wetness, but a terrible itchiness then began to suddenly torment Gloinn, and his only solution was to clench his buttocks together like Posh Spice and David Beckham making up after a fight.* When the Pope entered the room, accompanied by Cardinal O'Fiach, I felt immensely proud of my role in bringing this great character to the Irish

* Thanks to my granddaughter Duirbheuiannuineonn for this analogy drawn from popular culture.

people. I was truly 'on top of the world, looking down on creation'. But then an unfortunate personal disaster ensued which was to have the effect of rather souring the day for me also. Very unluckily, possibly due to nervousness, I involuntarily emitted a small 'fart' mere moments before my introduction. Initially, I was greatly relieved that my 'unwelcome guest' was of the silent variety, but there followed anxious moments of heightened tension while I awaited to see if it would be pungent. To my absolute horror, in a matter of seconds, I was aware of an odour reminiscent of a cattle sale in Kells. I hurriedly considered quickly changing places with Larry so that he could take the blame, but before I could act on my plan, I found myself locked in polite conversation with the Holy Father. Obviously, though of course he very kindly didn't remark on the fact, we both knew that I was the cause of the foul stench hanging in the air. I was so aware of the tense atmosphere brought about by my emission that I couldn't actually concentrate on what the great man was saying to me. (I found it difficult to understand him, anyway, with his bizarre accent. Was he speaking Polish or English? Or even Irish? I didn't know.) I just wanted the unpleasant aroma to go away as quickly as possible. Trying to maintain an exterior appearance of calm, I was unable to do little but smile and occasionally nod my head in agreement with whatever the Pontiff was talking about. To be honest, I was so disorientated by the situation that I was relieved when he moved on to Gloinn. But poor old Mr McT. was in an even worse state than me. I'll never forget the look of sheer agony on his face when he was introduced. I just *knew* that if he hadn't been in such difficulty, he would have chatted away to JP (II) for ages, but judging by his expression his only thought was 'how soon can I get to the toilet?' Our meeting with God's Representative on Earth/Maynooth seemed to be over in a flash, and while I felt – along with some obvious embarrassment – a genuine, wonderful sense of serenity after the world famous Pole left to go to the disco downstairs, Gloinn's only thought was to get to the jacks. When he returned a few minutes later he was *furious*. 'Of all the times it had to happen!' he said over and over again. His day had been completely ruined. Nevertheless, largely through our own efforts, we had at least got to meet a living Pope in Ireland. (Larry was literally struck dumb with the momentousness of the event and needed on the spot medical attention.) I personally feel it has been one of the major achievements of my life.

An entertaining footnote: I happened to be reminiscing about the great day with Gloinn a year or two later, when I discovered to my immense amusement that he was under the impression that it was the Holy Father who had 'let one go'. At the time of writing I still haven't corrected my old friend on this point!

CHAPTER 9

Angela's Gnashers

After the papal visit, Catholicism went through a boom period. Vocations went up by 50 per cent (three young men applied to join the priesthood in the six-month period immediately afterwards) and the trend in not going to mass was reversed. Sadly though, these were not long-term consequences, and the onslaught of atheism was not held off for long. The new decade would be the most testing yet for traditional Catholicism. There were highlights, of course. The Anti-Abortion Amendment of 1983 was comfortably passed, although by that year contraception had become available in the country for the first time in the shape of 'johnnies' and 'fanny magnets'. I remember being on a television programme during this period when I confused a Students Union representative from Trinity College by agreeing with her about contraception. This girl, who was called Concepta – I deliberately referred to as 'Contracepta', which drove her mad – was very puzzled by my statement. 'Oh, yes,' I said, 'I'm fully in favour of contraception, Contracepta.' But then of course I explained that I thought the best form of contraception was not to have sex at all! Gloinn was watching at home, and when he heard this, he told me later, he nearly died with the laughter! My very funny argument was based on the fact that not having sex was basically the best form of contraception because then there was no way that anyone could get pregnant. (I just hoped the presenter wouldn't bring up the rogue example of Noreen.) Of course, I was being slightly disingenuous, but I knew that there was a certain logic to my argument, and that it would give people watching at home who hated students (basically everyone in the country) a great laugh. All my friends who saw me on the programme thought I was just hilarious, and that I had made a real fool of the girl from Trinity.

Later, I tried to get a videotape of the show from RTE and was very disappointed to find out that the original programme had been 'wiped'.

Noreen's health by this time was failing badly. Doctor Sweetman told me that she was on her 'last legs' and that she could 'pop her clogs' at any moment. Naturally he gave me this news at the worst possible time: just before I was to go to Scotland for the first combined euthanasia/abortion/artificial insemination conference hosted by Father Liam Stack. Father Stack was a very popular veteran of the euthanasia/abortion/artificial insemination scene and was known as 'the fun-loving Jesuit'. As a great bonus, entertainment was to be provided by the Liverpool/Irish comedian Tom O'Connor, whose brand of bawdy but 'knowing' vulgarity had always appealed to me when I'd seen him on television. Father Stack, a tremendous entertainer in his own right, was just the man to host an event of this type, as there is always a tendency that discussions about euthanasia, abortion and artificial insemination can get very serious. Gloinn always looked forward to these jaunts, as, more often than not, there was a 'free bar' after the day's discussion, and one could drink pints of porter and all types of spirits until the early hours for absolutely nothing. I was blowed if I was going to let Noreen put the kybosh on what looked like being an absolutely fabulous weekend.

We checked into a hotel in Ayrshire on a beautiful July evening after flying over from Dublin. I was delighted to see that Jimmy 'Kiss of Life' Traynor, an old pal of mine from the Department of Welfare (from where I'd retired in 1977), was also staying in the hotel, and we had a great chat about the old days there. Jimmy was known as 'Kiss of Life' because of his fierce opposition to euthanasia. He would go around hospitals, accusing doctors and nurses of not doing enough to keep the patients alive, and causing a lot of trouble for them. His attempts to give 'kisses of life' to the dying were well meaning, but in the end he probably caused more deaths than he saved lives. He eventually ended up being barred from every hospital in Dublin. I also think that Jimmy had got it into his head that practically everybody who died in hospital was a victim of euthanasia. I asked him whether he was looking forward to the abortion and artificial insemination part of the conference, and I remember he got very haughty, saying that 'he wouldn't be interested in that stuff'. Euthanasia was his 'bag', and that was all there was to it, although when I said I thought that there was a definite euthanasia aspect to abortion, his ears pricked up a little. (I must admit that I have never shared Jimmy's enthusiasm for the euthanasia issue, as I have always regarded it as being at the less fashionable, or 'sexy', end of the traditional-values/catholic-interest/morality spectrum.) After a great chat about the old times and some of the marvellous characters we had known, he left my room, but we agreed to meet in the bar later that evening for a few 7-Ups (Jimmy, like myself, was a lifelong teetotaller). I was very happy at this stage, and eagerly looking forward to the first discussion group of the weekend, to be hosted the next morning by Father Stack, who Jimmy told me had been in absolutely cracking form at an exclusively euthanasia-themed event in Sheffield a few weeks previously (apparently, he had had his audience in stitches throughout!). But then the phone rang. Of course, I knew that it would be Doctor Sweetman with bad news about Noreen. Sure enough, I was right. Sweetman informed me that she had died twenty minutes before. Of all the inconveniences that she had caused me over the years, this surely took the biscuit. Not alone would I have to miss the conference, but airline tickets would have to be changed, funeral arrangements would have to be made, and I would be obliged to organize another reception in the Glenworth, which would of course cost me a lot of money. But, like so often in life, it was a case of just 'having to get on with it'. What really annoyed me on the day of the funeral was the fact that I was told by the manager of the hotel that a room in the Glenworth and a meal for twenty people would cost eighty pounds. Of course, I thought all drinks would be included in the price, but I was informed (*after* the bar had closed) that only the Guinness was free, and that I would have to pay an extra bar bill of one hundred and fifty pounds. I went home from the hotel *furious* and swore that they would never have my custom again.

My retirement opened up many new opportunities for me, and I was determined to spend it in as productive a way as possible. I had seen many other elderly gents 'go to seed' after they had stopped working, and I was determined that was something which was not going to happen to me. Working on *Catholicism Today* was very much like a whole new career anyway, and as Gloinn himself had also retired at this stage (although in his case writing books and novels had more or less become a full-time job) I suggested that we should rent a small office together. He agreed with me immediately, and before long we were producing the magazine from a small room over a fishing-tackle shop in Ringsend. At this time we were involved in a lot of correspondence, and it wasn't long before the workload began getting a bit too much for us. Gloinn suggested that we take on a secretary, and I readily agreed. Gloinn oversaw the inter-view process, I was in America for a few weeks visiting Father Sean Fagan, the Cherokee Indian priest with the Irish-sounding name, and by the time I'd returned, there was a lovely girl working in the office called Oonagh. Things seemed to be going along happily enough, until one day I came into the room and saw Gloinn sitting in his chair looking very glum. Oonagh was nowhere to be

seen. I made Gloinn and myself a cup of tea and enquired if anything unusual had happened. I thought he
might have been annoyed because he had recently been
having trouble with a builder who had tried to charge
him almost half a million pounds for fixing a leak in his
roof (original estimate: sixty quid). No, he said, that
wasn't what he was concerned about. Was it something
to do with Oonagh, then? He nodded gravely, then
asked me if I'd ever heard of a thing called 'sexual
harassment'. I said to him that it was a phrase that I
thought I'd heard on the news, but I really didn't know
what it was. It sounded like the name of a quiz programme on Channel 4. No, no, said Gloinn, it was a
very different thing entirely. He told me that Oonagh
had taken a notion into her head that Gloinn had done
something which could be covered by this term, and
that she was going to take him to court over it. I asked
him if there was any particular incident which might
have caused her to resort to this course of action, and he
said that he'd been racking his brains about it, but he
honestly couldn't think of a single thing. The *only* incident which he could remember, and to his mind it was
completely harmless, was when he'd been sunbathing
on the roof in his swimming trunks and he'd spotted
some dirt at the top of one of his legs. For some reason,
maybe because of his arthritis, his arms had become
paralysed, so he asked Oonagh if she'd mind wiping the
dirt off. While she was doing this, his swimming trunks
fell down, and he found himself standing nude in front
of her. There were maybe one or two minor details as

well which he didn't think were of much significance. 'Oh, yes,' he suddenly remembered, 'there was something I said about polishing a doorknob that she might have misunderstood.' But we both agreed there was really nothing untoward or 'out of order' about the incident. I knew that relations between Gloinn and Oonagh were usually very good, and I'd often see him having a laugh with her, making funny remarks about her breasts.

The three-month jail sentence came as something of a surprise to both of us, but Gloinn kept his spirits up well when he was 'inside', and in fact became something of a 'shark' at the popular prison pursuit of pool playing. I visited him regularly in Mountjoy, where he wrote a 'jail journal' which still remains unpublished, although in my view it's quite brilliant and doesn't glamorize the prison experience in the way that films like *The Great Escape* or *Schindler's List* do. Because Gloinn preferred watching history documentaries or Irish-language programmes to *Coronation Street* on the television, he acquired the nickname 'The Professor' amongst the prisoners, which I think secretly quite pleased him. (I too, because of my frequent visits 'inside', was given a nickname by the cons: 'Bum Wrap'. Even today I will occasionally call Gloinn 'The Professor' just to annoy him! Needless to say, he will respond with an immediate 'What are you saying there, Bum Wrap?) It was also in Mountjoy that we first met Father Barry Hourican, a lovely gentle priest who had quite wrongly been convicted of arms and sex offences. On Gloinn's release, my old friend and I decided to campaign for justice for Father Hourican, and sure enough, the elderly cleric was soon let go on account of 'health problems', although I'm sure our efforts on his behalf did not go unnoticed. He would burst back into the headlines in 1998, but I will tell that part of his story towards the end of this book.

Myself and Gloinn's interest in television has dwindled in recent years because of the fact that television programmes now are all shite. Although never compulsive viewers, both of us in the past would always watch programmes about religious (e.g. Catholic) faith, the Irish language and historical documentaries. Sadly, this type of fare has become rarer and rarer as the TV bosses feed us an endless diet of quiz shows, cookery programmes and 'soaps' featuring members of ethnic minorities in unrealistically prominent roles. My ideal TV channel would feature programmes about Irish-speaking priests who are members of the Gaelic Athletic Association, dislike Protestants, promote celibacy, take a strong line against abortion and contraception, and are uncompromising physical-force nationalists. Is it too much to ask, especially in our new 'digital age', for a channel exclusively devoted to this kind of programme?

Father Joe Collins, before he succumbed to alcohol poisoning in the Glenworth, once told me the greatest argument I've ever heard against divorce. We were having a very interesting chat about the subject one day as we walked out on the Hill of Howth overlooking Dublin

Bay. His wisdom was so evident and impressive on the subject that I would like to reprint here our conversation, as I recall it, to give the full flavour of his argument (*I think the tone of our conversation is very much in the style of a wise master instructing a willing, but as yet somewhat innocent, young pupil*):

'Another word for divorce, Eoin, is re-marriage. Now, Eoin, tell me, what are the other main events, apart from marriage, that a human being, man or woman, goes through?'

'I would say the answer to that question would be "birth and death", Father.'

'That's right, Eoin. "Births, marriages and deaths"; it's one of the most familiar phrases in the English language. Now, tell me, Eoin, if I put the prefix "re" before the words "birth" and "death", what would you have? Tell me now, like a good man.'

'You would have the words "re-birth" and "re-death", Father.'

'That's right. Now, what does each of them mean?'

'Well, "re-birth" would mean being born more than once. And "re-death" would mean dying more than once.'

'And tell me, Eoin, can a man or a woman be born more than once or die more than once?'

'No, Father, they cannot.'

'That's right. You can't put the prefix "re" before "birth" and "death" because it makes words that just don't make any sense. Now, Eoin, if we can't put the prefix "re" before "birth" and "death", do you think it would be right to put it before the word "marriage"?'

'I have to say, Father, I don't think it would.'

The sheer simplicity and logic of his argument has stayed with me for years. The whole idea of "re-marriage" is plainly ridiculous. During the divorce referendum of 1987, it was an argument I used over and over again against the bearded intellectuals and feminesbians. Needless to say, the people were 'with us all the way', and the spectre of marital break-up was kept on hold for another decade.

The mid-1980s were very dark years, and it was always great to have a laugh amidst all the gloom. A very funny programme on RTE at the time was a *Candid Camera*-type show hosted by Mike Murphy, where ordinary members of the public would be 'caught out' by Mike and his team. One day I was watching the show, when to my great surprise, followed by equally great amusement, I realized that Gloinn was about to become the hapless victim of one of Mr Murphy's madcap set-ups! Mike was pretending to be a policeman stopping motorists to check to see if their road tax was up to date, but when the car stopped, some of the other members of the production team would go round the back of the vehicle and attach a giant anchor to the back bumper. The driver would then attempt to drive off, but of course because of the anchor, would be unable to go anywhere. Mike would then pretend he didn't know what was happening, while the driver got out of the car to

investigate. Mr Murphy fooled a couple of motorists like this, and it was very funny to see the drivers' reaction at being unable to drive off, and then their utter bemusement when they saw the anchor. This was very enjoyable stuff, but when I saw Gloinn's brown Ford Escort drive into shot, I nearly died! It was a pity I didn't have a video recorder in those days, because I certainly would have taped what happened next. Gloinn's encounter with the 'Guard' went something like this:

Guard: (*Mike Murphy, putting on a country accent*) Just checking your tax there . . . Where are you off to, sir?

Gloinn: A conference on celibacy and an equitable tax system.

This was an annual event held in Dundalk that Gloinn always went to.

Guard: Your tax is all right there anyway. Off you go, sir, and have a nice journey.

Gloinn: Thank you, Guard.

Gloinn, of course, then tried to drive off, but couldn't because of the anchor tied to his back bumper. I could see that he was getting very frustrated!

Gloinn: What the hell is wrong with this car?!

Guard: (*Knowing very well what the problem is!*) Is there something the matter, sir? Why are you not able to drive off?

Gloinn: The car won't go! What the f*** is going on?!

Gloinn tends to swear a lot when he gets angry, and I just knew, in his frustration, that the air was going to turn the blue!

Guard: Are you all right there, sir?

Gloinn: For f***'s sake! The shaggin' car's gone mad! F***! F***! F***!

Gloinn, at Mike's instigation, then went round to the back of the car to see what the problem was. Needless to say, the look on his face when he saw the anchor was absolutely priceless! He didn't know *what* had happened!? How on God's earth had this thing got on to the car? Eventually, after some *shocking* language from Gloinn, Mike told him that he'd been set up, and my old friend suddenly went very sheepish indeed, looking around to see if he could find the hidden camera and hiding his face. It was very, very funny to watch. Needless to say, the next time I saw him, I slagged him off mercilessly, but he didn't seem to take it very well, and told me after a while in no uncertain terms to drop the subject. Still, it was something I enjoyed enormously, and was disappointed to discover when I contacted RTE recently to get a copy of the tape, that the show had been 'wiped'.

Catholicism Today, which had done its job by promoting the idea of a papal visit, was now 'laid to rest', but as we approached the 1990s, which would be one of the last decades of the twentieth century, we launched another magazine, *Majority Ethos*. Gloinn and myself were determined that our new publication would be a hard-hitting antidote to the, by now, almost pervasive liberalism in the media. The launch of the magazine was timed to coincide with the local elections, and before voting day we put out 'feelers' to other Catholic family-oriented political parties, with a view to forming a loose alliance of similarly minded groups. (With typical hostility, *The Irish Times* referred to our proposed group as a 'rainbow coalition of eejits'.) We were particularly interested in one organization, the Catholic Family Party (CFP), but were rather disappointed and somewhat surprised to discover that their proposed candidate was a woman with two young children! It seemed unusual that a lady who believed in family values would jeopardize the future of her offspring by abandoning them for the cut and thrust of the debating chamber. What use is a well-constructed argument against air pollution if one's children are running wild in the house sticking jam into video recorders and eating coal? In the end, no formal links were established between myself and Gloinn and the Christian parties.

We were keen to make *Majority Ethos* a 'fun' magazine, and steer it away from the 'fuddy-duddy' image that had bedevilled so many Catholic magazines in the past. To this end we introduced a light-hearted Catholic cross-word, a problem page (no questions about sex; 'I'm too fat' – that type of thing), and a regular television-review column written by Gloinn's niece Angela (she hated *everything*!). We were keen to have the support of the Bishops for our new venture, and I also wrote to the new Papal Nuncio, Doctor Birindini, asking him if he would like to contribute a regular piece on any subject of his choice. I was very pleased when he replied almost immediately, saying that he would love to write a monthly column on his favourite hobby (after religion, of course), which turned out to be, rather surprisingly, motor racing. It wasn't exactly what I had in mind, but a regular column from a Papal Nuncio, no matter what topic he chooses to write about, is certainly nothing to be sneezed at. We agreed to meet to discuss terms in Kerry, where the Nuncio was holidaying with a few (non-religious) friends from Rome. Doctor Birindini turned out to be a lovely man, very much in the style of the fat, jolly, Italian clergyman so familiar from American gangster films of the 1970s. Our meeting happened to coincide with the Rose of Tralee festival, a celebration of girls, both native to Ireland and of Irish extraction, held annually in the picturesque southern town. Gay Byrne was usually the host of the event, and he always handled the affair with typical professionalism. An important part of the contest always took place just before the girls met 'Gaybo', when they would be checked by a doctor and a priest to confirm that they were virgins behind a sheet to the side of the stage.

As we were in the locality, we decided to pop along for the second night of the competition. I have to say it was great fun, and I remember Doctor Birindini made no apologies for heartily cheering on the Italian Rose (parents from Roscommon and Mayo)! During the break, the Nuncio decided to go to the toilet as he was 'bursting', and as I always enjoy occasions more when I have the security of an empty bladder, I decided to accompany him. But we couldn't find a 'men's room', as Doctor Birindini referred to it (he had spent some years in the US) anywhere. There were precious few signs up, and when we asked directions, we seemed to invariably end up at the Ladies. After another wild goose chase where we found ourselves beside yet another beer tent, the situation was becoming perilous. Doctor Birindini had gone bright red in the face, and looked as though he couldn't hold it in for much longer. (I was fine at this stage, as I had had only a couple of 7-Ups, whereas the Nuncio had been drinking pints of Guinness since mid-afternoon.) It looked as though his only hope was to sneak into the Ladies. If caught, his plan was to pretend to be a lady, and use his Papal Nuncio 'frock' as evidence to support his claim. This was a plan which I thought was unlikely to work, as the Nuncio was as bald as a coot, and the only lady he would pass for would be one suffering from the worst case of alopecia in the history of ladies' hair loss. I quickly dissuaded him from this plan, advising that if he just explained to any lady who questioned his right to be there that he was the Papal Nuncio and that he'd just been 'caught short', they would certainly understand. It was the type of thing that could happen to anybody. I, of course, agreed to 'keep watch'. The Nuncio sneaked inside, and all was going to plan until I saw a lady approaching fast, making a beeline for the toilet. I recognized her immediately as Mary Doorly-Blount, the eccentric and ill-tempered spinster food critic of *The Irish Times*, who famously lived alone with fifteen cats. This was a stroke of very bad luck. Myself and Gloinn knew from a 'mole' inside *The Irish Times* that it was their editorial policy to embarrass and degrade members of the Hierarchy at every opportunity. Ominously, this looked like an ideal situation. Despite the fact that she was only the newspaper's food critic, Doorly-Blount would no doubt report the incident to her editor who would in all likelihood splash it all over the feature pages. I had to think on my feet, and I immediately came up with a ruse which happily worked very well. 'Are you Mary Doorly-Blount?' I enquired. The shambolically dressed (slacks, dark glasses, crumpled grey cardigan with red wine stains) hack nodded, and I immediately launched into a ferocious attack on the food in the restaurant of a local hotel, which was completely unjustified as I'd eaten there recently and the fare was gorgeous. It just happened to be the first name of a hotel that popped into my head. Food critics are always on the lookout to slag off restaurants, so she was very interested in my stinging criticism. For good measure, I also told her the wine had been overpriced (I've never drunk wine in my life!). I was delighted when she then produced a notebook from her handbag and started writing in it, as this would distract her even more from the door of the lavatory. Sure enough, she never noticed Doctor Birindini's exit, and when he arrived at my side, looking much happier than he'd been a few minutes earlier, Doorly-Blount was still buried in her notebook. Myself and the Nuncio then made our excuses and left, thanking our lucky stars for such a fortuitous escape.

As an amusing footnote to the story, Doorly-Blount later wrote a review of the restaurant I had complained about. Nearly everything I'd said she reported word for word!

I remember our time together in Kerry being dogged by Frank McCourt-like bad weather. The Papal Nuncio, who was originally from Naples, was absolutely bamboozled by the amount of rain that fell on modern Ireland and it was a constant topic of conversation with him. His initial enthusiasm at being appointed to a 'safe' Catholic country was now fading as fast as his suntan. 'What is going on with the weather in your island home, Eoin?' he would ask me, with a look of utter bemusement on his angelic face as he clung on to his big regulation-issue black umbrella, the sound of the giant raindrops pummelling into the 'brolly' almost drowning out our conversation. 'You know, if we had this kind of thing in Italia, people would fear it was the end of the world.' It was a telling comment, coming from someone who had grown up in the shadow of Mount Vesuvius. I am no meteorologist, and I was unable to give a reason for the constant downpour. I think I might have said something to the effect that 'Oh, it's just God's plan for us,' but the Nuncio seemed unconvinced. In my experience, his reaction was typical of many churchmen when lay people like myself try to explain the irrational using the 'God's plan' argument. They raise an eyebrow and look at you as if you're slightly bonkers. My sister Grainne, who emigrated to the US in 1940, once asked the Archbishop of Cincinnati a vaguely theological question to which he replied, 'Look, lady, I don't know much about that stuff. I'm just doing a job here.' Anyway, no rational argument could explain the rain to the roly-poly Neapolitan.

Often I see satellite weather maps on the news. Nearly always, clear skies allow us to make out the familiar green

form of the European continent. Ireland, however, is invariably enveloped in cloud which has formed a perfectly shaped mirror image of the land form underneath; a sort of snugly fitting 'cloud hat', if you like. It is not even unusual to see that the entire *planet* is clear of cloud – except perhaps for swirly bits around the North and South Poles – while our own unhappy isle is cocooned under a thick grey mush. It is no wonder that the mood of the people is generally grim, lightened only by alcoholism and occasional wins in the Eurovision Song Contest.

Censorship in Ireland, since my time on the Censorship Board, had gone to hell by the 1990s. Basically, everything was allowed, and it was almost impossible to stem the flow of filth coming at us from all sides. It would have been a Herculean task to alert the authorities to every single film, book and play that was polluting the country, but one thing I was determined should not be allowed anywhere near the public was a recently published novel by our old 'friend' [*author's quotation marks*] Ranger MacWoods. Since *Big Jugs* and *Fill up me Johnnies* many years before, MacWoods had continued his filthy work, and his name would occasionally pop up in connection with a disgusting play or book which was guaranteed to offend. Nine times out of ten, this stuff would have been banned in the days when I was alive, but with the increase of liberalism, less and less obstacles were being put in his path. By 1995 his novel *Pork Tribunal* had been published by a small publishing house in Arklow, and it was brought to my attention by a neighbour of mine, Finbar Walsh. When I read a copy, I could scarcely believe that such sheer 'shit' could be printed, and I decided to embark on a private prosecution of MacWoods for obscenity.

Pork Tribunal is offensive in countless ways. The hugely unbelievable scenario concerns a homosexual love affair between two Irish Members of Parliament, Donal Geraghty (Fine Gael) and Pascal Clonliffe (Fianna Fail), set against the background of an investigation into irregularities concerning the siting of a pork factory. MacWoods' numerous pornographic descriptions of 'gay' sex involving male TDs reached a new low in publishing. Here, for example, is the opening passage (*ladies may wish at this stage to skip ahead a few pages*):

'Fuck, fuck, fuck me up the arse, you baldy fucker!'

He sprawled all over him, thrusting his hot member up the youth's arse until he came with a loud 'whoosh'. 'Eeurgh . . .' moaned the youth. Pascal rolled on to his side, and as his head hit the sheets, he got a full view of his companion's red raw arse, blistered and surrounded by a ruddy pink rash, which both disgusted and enthralled him. He knew that Frankie, the boy of seventeen who lay next to him, would pause for a while and then start barking the commands which befitted his 'master' role. This, of course, made Pascal the servant, which did not thrill him as much, but pleased Frankie immensely. It was a game they played together. One of many, Pascal thought to himself, not for the first time.

'Go out and get me a box of Smarties.'

Pascal paused for a while, unwilling to seem too subservient. This would infuriate Frankie.

> *'Go out and get me a box of Smarties, you baldy fucker!'*
> *It was a phrase which the youth used again and again to*
> *taunt Pascal. 'You baldy fucker'.*

It is scarcely conceivable that someone would compose such rubbish. It even gets worse, with the Fine Gael TD having lurid erotic fantasies about the (admittedly very attractive) Sinn Fein leader Gerry Adams and having an affair with a young Belgian. But the most disturbing passages describe homosexual 'love' between the two main protagonists. Here is another absolutely revolting example:

> *That night he went to Donal's place again. Their love-making was as exciting as ever. They lost themselves completely in sexual ecstasy the like of which Pascal had never known in all his life. At one point, just as Pascal thought he was about to explode, Donal asked him to do something that no one had ever asked him to do before.*
> *'Pascal, could you stick your head up my arse?'*
> *'What? Sorry, Donal?'*
> *'It's just . . . I've noticed . . . you've got a very small head.'*
> *Ah! That was what Gerry Giles, the man who had fitted his wig, had said. Other people had remarked on his small head as well. It must be very noticeable. Donal continued, 'It would be so brilliant. There's some oil on the table. Use it for lubrication.'*
> *Pascal, not unnaturally, even though he was hugely sexually excited, had to think about this for a second. Sticking his head up someone else's arse. That was really 'pushing the boat out'. Even in San Francisco they'd probably have to think twice about that one. But eventually, because he thought Donal was just great, he relented. He got the*

baby oil from the bedside table, and massaged Donal's hole with it. Just in the nick of time, he remembered at the last moment to remove his wig. Then he took a deep breath and 'went for it'. He shoved his head up Donal's arse as far as he could go while the Fine Gael man screamed with pleasure. Eventually his whole head was submerged by Donal's insides. Pascal decided to open his eyes and have a look around – this, after all, was an experience he was unlikely to repeat – but his lids were pressed up against some indeterminate fleshy substance and would not open. Anyhow, he probably would have been unable to see anything in the darkness. Eventually, he could hold his breath no more, and withdrew from his lover. My God, that had been incredible. Donal was beside himself with joy. 'Thank you, Pascal. That was great fun.' In gratitude, Donal gave Pascal a delicious blow job.

The idea of two TDs getting up to this kind of thing is, of course, utterly fantastic.

MacWoods, showing contempt for the Irish people at every turn, sets out to sensationalize and shock, knowing that a 'quick buck' can always be made by pandering to people's most base instincts. This stuff even makes garbage like *Father Ted* (another ludicrous depiction of the Irish) look intelligent! My private prosecution of MacWoods in the end came to nothing, as I simply could not afford the huge legal costs involved. However, the fact that this is now the kind of artefact coming out of the 'land of saints and scholars' is surely a measure of how low we have sunk.

In 1998, Father Barry Hourican, Gloinn's fellow prisoner in Mountjoy some years before, was re-arrested on arms and sex offences and detained in the political/ paedophile wing of Portlaoise prison. Despite the overwhelming evidence against him, both myself and Gloinn believed that, even if he was guilty, he should be released because he was a priest. Our letters to the newspapers appealed strongly to people's folk memory of the tradition of the Republican Paedophile Priest, which I discussed in an earlier chapter. The campaign to free Father Barry, which we directed from Gloinn's house in Naas, was going exceedingly well, and we had just put our feet up after a hectic day of phone calls and letter writing, when we heard a frantic knocking on the door. Gloinn went to open it, and was more than surprised to discover a dishevelled and extremely agitated Father Hourican standing outside. Obviously in a state of heightened anxiety, he told us that he'd escaped from Portlaoise, and was now 'on the run'. We ushered the old priest in, sat him down at Gloinn's kitchen table and gave him a cup of tea and a long rectangular pink biscuit which crumbled in his fingers as he ate it; more from the shaking of his hand than the wafer-like texture of the fancy. He was almost completely covered in mud, as he had dug a tunnel out of the prison with some fellow Republican paedophiles, and because it was a wet night, the soil had turned to a mucky sludge. We pondered what to do. Father Hourican asked Gloinn if he had a cellar, as it was a tradition to hide runaway priests in cellars. Unfortunately, Gloinn had filled in his cellar with cement some years before for 'structural' reasons (in reality a tax dodge). After much discussion, I eventually came up with a plan which I thought was foolproof. As the Gardai were on the lookout for a priest, if we dressed Father Hourican in 'civilian' clothes and claimed that he was my brother on a visit from Canada, then in all likelihood the elderly cleric would be able to take refuge with me and avoid detection until he could be spirited away to South America. There he could join the well established Vatican 'escape route' for bothersome priests who had embarrassed Rome, such as the recently disgraced playboy Archbishop of Galway, Eamonn Casey. After a headline making, peacock-like display of sexual exhibitionism which had resulted in the birth of a son, Bishop Casey had ended up in Ecuador or some equally unlikely place of refuge. 'Perhaps I could teach boys in a small village in the rainforest,' said Father Hourican, his face lighting up for the first time that evening. Alas, our plan was soon foiled. The Guards were 'hot on the trail' of the fugitive nationalist/sex offender, and, as so often happens in the more popular type of detective novel, his muddy footprints were a dead giveaway. Fifteen burly policemen burst in through the door before any of us had time to react (the three of us were, after all, octogenarians) and in seconds had the poor ould RPP pinned to the floor where they proceeded to give him a bit of a 'roughing up'. Regarding myself and Gloinn's role in the affair, charges were never pressed on account of our great age, and the whole episode turned out to be merely a diverting incident in our (by then obviously doomed) quest to secure the release of Father Barry.

CHAPTER 10

Through Baltinglass, Darkly

And so, here we are, in the Ireland of the new millennium. Whereas in my youth, life was a perilous occupation, and most of the time we seemed to be hanging on for dear life against the ravages of disease and poverty, nowadays the main danger comes from being run over by ten-year-olds wearing Manchester United jerseys. There is precious little left of the Ireland of my youth, except for Gloinn and the constant begrudgery. The country as I first knew it is dead and gone. It is not just the trams; not just the piety of the people, nor their unquestioning respect for their elders and people in authority; not just the dominant figure of Admiral Nelson staring down at the people from the top of his column in the middle of O'Connell Street. It's a *feeling* that has disappeared; something that cannot be described in mere words. Gloinn, some years ago, was determined to write a book about Dublin before 1960. He rented a small cottage for a month in Donegal; arrived there with his typewriter; and gave up in five minutes. The task, quite simply, proved impossible.

I am a very old man now, and at the beginning of 1999 I suffered a very severe stroke. Thankfully, Sorcha and her husband Senan have been a great help to me, but as it became more and more difficult to continue living in my own house, without running the risk of scalding myself or setting the place on fire, I agreed with my daughter that it would be best if I saw out my final days in a nursing home. She knew of a perfect place, in Connemara, not far from my old Irish College at St Fionn's, where her father-in-law's life had ebbed away in an atmosphere of overwhelming peace and serenity, to the point where he really hated having to die and leave the place behind. At first, though, maybe because I am old and set in my ways, I was a little nervous at the prospect. But when I saw the beautiful and awe-inspiring building of St Columbana's for the first time on a sunny evening in July, I knew I would be happy here. It is run by Brigidine nuns, and I liked very much the idea of seeing out my final days amongst these very special 'ladies', who had been responsible for my early schooling, and from whom I had learnt so much. A nun who taught me when I was perhaps five or six years old, Sister Ignatius (or Sister 'Pugnacious' as she was called by some of the older boys), once told me a story about a little yellow duck. I have always remembered it. This duck had no friends, and it would follow the other ducks in his pond at a distance, because it was very shy and lonely. I always thought that this was a beautiful story, and while it has no relevance to my own life, it conjures up a vivid image of a shy duck.

Gloinn, who lives nearby, often visits with Maire. My oldest friend is ninety-one now, and Maire eighty-eight. While most elderly women shrivel to a familiar Mother

Theresa dried prune-like form, Maire still weighs in at a heady twenty stone. Gloinn, at the time of writing, due to a recent chest operation which went badly wrong, is now down to barely three stone, and resembles a tiny child. The doctors have given him two scenarios: in time he may regain weight, get back to his normal hearty self and be able to carry on as he did before his illness; or he may die a slow and agonizing death. While getting out of the car on his last visit to St Columbana's, a gust of wind blew him across the gravelled forecourt and into a ditch where he remained for several hours until discovered by the gardener. He has become quite transparent, and when he stands in front of a bright light, it is possible to literally see through him. ('I've been able to see through him for years!' Maire noted on a recent visit. It was a very funny remark, perhaps the only one she's ever made in the sixty years of her marriage.) Surprisingly, Gloinn's sex drive remains as great as it has always been ('I'm still mad for it, Eoin!') and after relieving himself into his sofa, he can lose up to a fifth of his body weight. Maire still drives him completely mental, and recently I joked that with the new divorce legislation, maybe the time was right for him to make a break for it! I was surprised that a smile did not break out on his face, and I could see by his pensive gaze that he was taking my suggestion more seriously than I had intended. Maire once told Noreen that after an argument with Gloinn, he had told her he believed that their marriage had run its course. Very calmly, he turned to his wife and said, 'I have wings, I want to fly.' Of course, nothing became of it in the end. In his heart he knew that he would be stuck with her for all time.

He remains stoic throughout all his problems. 'Wasn't it a stroke of luck that I was born an Irish Catholic,' he said to me recently. 'I couldn't imagine meself as a Hindu or a Muslim or one of thoses foreign lads.' He was absolutely right. And sure where could he get a decent pint of Guinness in Kurdistan?! He regrets the fact that he never married (or even met) Sophia Loren. It is amusing for me to picture the lovely Italian star of – well, I can't think of any of her films – as 'Mrs Gloinn McTire', and sometimes the idea makes me almost double up with laughter. I said to Gloinn many years ago around the late 1930s when he had a similar crush on Bette Davis that the chances of him ending up married to Miss Davis were about as high as Maire landing the role of Scarlett O'Hara in *Gone with the Wind*! This was a very funny remark, but Gloinn topped it recently when he said that he reckoned it would have been more likely that in his lifetime he would have married Bette Davis, Sophia Loren, Marilyn Monroe and the entire chorus of the Ziegfeld Follies than Maire even getting as far as an audition for Scarlett O'Hara! I think I must have laughed at that remark for about two hours until my sides were absolutely aching!

I myself have not much time left in this world, something that perhaps certain people, if not most people, in the country will be happy about. Sadly, my inspiration for poetry seems to have deserted me, but that hardly surprises, as we are nowadays bereft of much that would have ignited the passions of the great bards of the past. My last poem, given away free with the last issue of *Majority Ethos*, is simply called *Memories*.

> *Memories of home,*
> *Silently transgressing the pastures of the past,*
> *All that is left of the grassy shack,*
> *Said the old man to the child,*
> *Is that bit over there.*

As Gloinn says, 'You still have it, Eoin!' But it is hard to find motivation when I see the bleakness of the modern world. A nun here at St Columbana's, Sister Majelleca, says that I should consider setting up my own Web site, and distributing my poetry on the Net, but I really wouldn't know where to start.

Just before my stroke, I attended a weekend of poetry reading in Fermanagh featuring many notable Northern Ireland poets. (Needless to say, the words 'glen' and 'vale', which one rarely hears in day-to-day life, featured in practically every poem!) I can never get enough of Northern Ireland poets, and do not subscribe to the proposal put forward by certain individuals that they should all be put up against a wall and shot. To my dismay, the weekend – which I generally enjoyed – was soured somewhat by a 'workshop' featuring feminesbian poetry, chaired by the Belfast feminesbian activist Orla Ni Suibh. I had come across Miss Ni Suibh once previously when she had written an

angry letter to *The Irish Press* in response to an article which Gloinn had penned entitled 'Why are Irish Girls so Ugly?'

In the olden days, a girl whose '**natural**' (?) [*author's brackets, question mark and bold type*] inclination was to lie with her own kind was hardly noticeable in society. There were, of course, tell-tale signs discernible in an individual: she would be unmarried and unattractive; she would live alone with her mother; she would dress badly and not bother much about personal appearance, and she would often sport a wispy moustache. But she was, overall, a quiet and harmless individual who most people felt sorry for. This older type of female 'same sexer' was not 'politicized', and was unaware that there was anything wrong with her except for the fact that she didn't like men. Generally, she boiled cabbage and carrots, rather than lentils and hummus. Nowadays, things are very different. The modern feminesbian is a vocal and abrasive propagandist for the overthrow of society. Illustrated handbooks and 'educational' videos demonstrating feminesbian sexual practices are freely distributed to schools while the media is dominated by feminesbian thinking (which even extends to our sports programmes). The presence of Miss Ni Suibh spoiled an otherwise excellent weekend of Northern Ireland poetry, and I hope that next year she will not be invited back by the organizers.

So, the little tugboat that has been my life is fast approaching the tranquil harbour that is death. I looked at myself in the mirror recently and found it strange to think that within a few years – if not months – or even weeks! – there would be grass growing through the eye sockets of my skull as my body decayed and returned to the dust that it had once been. (Although I must admit I have no memory of this previous 'dusty' state.)

I started off my story with an anecdote which described watching a video in the company of my friend, Father Bunny Long. Bunny has died since I wrote those words, and, very sadly, he did not pass away quietly in his bed, as I think would have been an appropriate and dignified end for such a lovely old cleric, but in a tragic and needless 'hit and run' motor accident outside his parochial house. Bunny was a simple man, and his dying words did not convey any great wisdom or insight into the human condition. In fact, because the first person on the scene of the accident was a parishioner whom Bunny had for some reason disliked, when this gentle-man offered his aid, Bunny told him to 'fuck off'. Sadly, these were the last words he uttered on earth. How unfortunate that such a kind and gentle priest should go out on such an untypical abrasive note. I hope that I shall be luckier when my time comes.

I like to think that even among those contemporaries and non-contemporaries who disagreed with my beliefs and values I have had some respect (although I know that I haven't) and an acknowledgement that, like Mr Sinatra, I have always done things 'swell'. It has been a long life, perhaps too long, but I wouldn't have been without it for the world.

THE OFFICIAL ORGAN OF THE CCCP · VOL 1 ISSUE 1 JULY 1991

MAJORITY ETHOS

MARRIAGE, NOT SEX · JOBS, NOT CONDOMS · FAITH, NOT SODOMY

QUIRKS OF QUOTAS AND BOUNDARIES LEAVE CHRISTIANS UNELECTED AS

3,000 DUBLINERS VOTE FOR OUR LORD

IN THIS ISSUE..

Page 2 -
■ Editorial Comment
■ Eoin O'Ceallaigh examines the Condom Crisis

Page 3 -
■ Gloinn Mac Tire chronicles the conception of the CCCP
■ Political booklet review - *Majority Ethos* outlines the historical dangers of supporting 'the left'

Page 4 -
■ Opinion - A call for greater Christian unity
■ Modern Woman - Not being ignored by the Hierarchy
■ 'Fun' Crossword for readers

Your View - Why not share your opinions on Christian/ political issues with *Majority Ethos* readers? Write today to: The Editor, *Majority Ethos*, interim address: 28 Cedar Court, Mount Tallant Avenue, Dublin 6 We look forward to hearing from you.

On June 27 the Dublin electorate gave the secular Haughey, Bruton and Socialist parties a clear message - ignore Christian Ireland at your peril; we want jobs, not condoms, for our children.

The near election of Sean Clerkin and Dominic Noonan, first time candidates in Cabra and Clontarf for the newly formed Christian Principles Party, is another nail in the twin coffins of both discredited international socialism and Haughey's new liberalism in Christian Ireland.

Refusal To Vote

The refusal of more than half of the Dublin electorate to turn out to vote for the parties of sodomy and condoms shows clearly that the Irish electorate will not be taken for fools. Yet those who voted found the electoral system inherently favoured the forces of darkness. The quirks of quotas and boundaries left Clerkin and Noonan unelected, despite

securing more votes than many liberals and socialists in other constituencies. This clear distortion of the wishes of the electorate is examined in our editorial inside.

Lord Mayor Outpolled

Predictably, the impact of the Christian parties was even greater than expected. In particular Clerkin and Noonan, with their combined mandate of 2,182 votes, would have outpolled such established liberal figures as outgoing Lord Mayor Michael Donnelly of Fianna Fail (only 1,985 in Rathmines), and Fine Gael's Jim 'Fixer' Mitchell (a mere 1,164 in Cabra).

Higgins Overwhelmed

In fact, even taken individually, either Clerkin (1,136 votes) or Noonan (1,048), would have overwhelmed both the well known Galway Socialist and friend of Marxist Nicaragua Michael 'D' Higgins (a miserly mandate of 940), whose chaotic campaign in Wicklow garnered a mere 642 votes.

Significantly, the combined vote for Clerkin and Noonan, along with running mates John O'Gorman (Artane) and Lily Fisher (Finglas), added to the votes of Harry Richards (Rathmines) and Eamon Murphy (Drumcondra) of the smaller Clan na bFinini family group, would have almost topped the 3,000 mark.

Electoral Collapse

This total would have overpowered such perennial poll-toppers as Richard Bruton (2,393 in Clontarf), brother of the latest architect of Fine Gael's ongoing electoral collapse, and Limerick Arch-Communist Jim Kemmy, whose meagre 1,418 votes is less than half of the Christian candidates' mandate in Dublin alone. The voice of the people has spoken - and that voice is the voice of Our Lord.

WHERE THE VOTES WENT IN DUBLIN

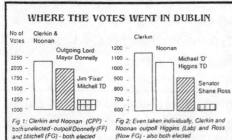

Fig 1: Clerkin and Noonan (CPP) - both unelected - outpoll Donnelly (FF) and Mitchell (FG) - both elected

Fig 2: Even taken individually, Clerkin and Noonan outpoll Higgins (Lab) and Ross (Now FG) - also both elected

'Majority Ethos': Gloinn and I tried to lose the 'fuddy duddy' image that had so bedevilled many other Catholic magazines.

Further Reading

Down, Up, and a Decade of the Rosary – The Christian Brothers and Bungee Jumping in Ireland, Desmond McKeeb (Trinity Press, Tralee, 1997).

Ireland in Crisis, Eoin O'Ceallaigh (Dunbeg Press, Cork, 1996).

By the Balls – The Story of My Capture and Torture by the Chinese Communists, Father Ned Rush (Dolphins Barn Press, Dublin, 1970).

The Lumpen Communist, Gloinn McTire (Dublin, 1939).

Counterblast, Gloinn McTire (Dublin, 1940).

Christ Almighty, Gloinn McTire (Dublin, 1940).

Ruthai Amach (Bicycles Outside), Eoin O'Ceallaigh (Dublin, 1939).

An Rogollach Buachaillearacht (The Rollicking Apron), Eoin O'Ceallaigh (Limbo Books, Limerick, 1975).

Mammy, I'd Rather Play with the Girls – Origins of Feminesbianism in Modern Ireland, Eoin O'Ceallaigh (Dunbeg Press, Cork, 1997).

The Man Behind the Third Reich, Gloinn McTire (Nationsozialismus Direkt!, Munchen, 1944).

Glossary for Foreign Readers

Fianna Fail – Popular Irish political party
Fine Gael – Less popular Irish political party
Riding – Sexual intercourse